BALTIMORE LIFE INSURANCE COMPANY

GENEALOGICAL ABSTRACTS

[MARYLAND]

Jerry M. Hynson

Introduction by
Sharon Ann Murphy
University of Virginia

HERITAGE BOOKS
2012

HERITAGE BOOKS
AN IMPRINT OF HERITAGE BOOKS, INC.

Books, CDs, and more—Worldwide

For our listing of thousands of titles see our website
at
www.HeritageBooks.com

Published 2012 by
HERITAGE BOOKS, INC.
Publishing Division
100 Railroad Ave. #104
Westminster, Maryland 21157

Copyright © 2004 Jerry M. Hynson

International Standard Book Numbers
Paperbound: 978-1-58549-930-4
Clothbound: 978-0-7884-8987-7

Contents

Introduction

Incorporated by the state of Maryland in December 1830, the Baltimore Life Insurance Company was among the first to actively sell life insurance in the United States, joining the Pennsylvania Company for Insurances on Lives and Granting Annuities (chartered 1812), the Massachusetts Hospital Life Insurance Company (1818), the New York Life Insurance and Trust Company (1830), and the Girard Life Insurance, Annuity and Trust Company of Pennsylvania (1836). (A sixth, the New England Mutual, was chartered in 1835 but did not begin issuing policies until 1843). The Baltimore Life sold their first policy in May 1831 and had only 25 policies on their books by the end of that year. But as early as 1833 the company was able to move into second place in the industry behind the New York Life Insurance and Trust Company, and by 1835 they possessed approximately 24% of the overall American market share.

The Baltimore Life was distinct from the other early companies for two main reasons. First, its location near the nation's capital, with Washington's growing bureaucratic workforce, provided the company with a potential customer base unique from that of the other major cities of the time. In March of 1833, the Baltimore Life officially opened an agency in the city of Washington, commissioning James H. Causten as its agent. Causten's main objective was to sell insurance policies to government clerks. In his acceptance letter dated March 31, 1833 he declared that he was "located in the midst of the public offices, & have an intimate acquaintance with nearly all the officers of the Departments, a class of persons of all others the best suited to the object of your Company." The Baltimore Life insured clerks in a wide array of government offices, including the state department, treasury department, circuit courts, solicitor's office, post office, land office, as well as many military personnel.

Second, the Baltimore Life was the only company positioned to sell life insurance in the South, although its business was largely confined to Maryland, Virginia, and Washington, D.C. While at least 5 other southern companies were organized between 1833 and 1836, none survived more than 4 years. Although several northern companies established agencies in the upper South, the Baltimore Life faced little serious competition for southern lives until the successful establishment of other life companies in the upper South beginning in the late 1840s, namely the Mutual Life Insurance Company of Maryland (1845-1857), the North Carolina Life (1849-1862) and the Greensboro Mutual Life Insurance & Trust Company (1853-1865). In particular, the Baltimore Life possessed a virtual monopoly on slave life insurance until the end of the 1840s. But reflecting the ambiguous designation of slaves as both person and property, the Baltimore Life eventually encountered competition for these risks not only from other life companies but from property insurance companies as well, including the Richmond Fire Association, the Asheville Mutual Insurance Company, and the Lynchburg Hose and Fire Insurance Company.

From their inception, the Baltimore Life received numerous inquiries regarding their willingness to insure the lives of slaves or valuable horses. One particularly interesting request came in March 1835 when the company's agent in Washington, James H. Causten, was solicited by the trustees of three orphanages to insure the life of a lion:

> The President of the United States
> [Andrew Jackson] has by authority
> of Congress made a donation to three
> orphan Asylums of this city of a
> Lion presented to him by the
> Emperor of Morocco. The trustees
> of these Asylums wish to secure the
> greatest benefit from the gift to said
> institutions, and have offered it for
> sale; $3000 in hand and an additional
> $1000 at the end of six years, if it
> live so long, has been offered for it;
> but the Trustees expect much more.
> In the mean time they wish to effect
> Insurance on its life, say for six
> months with the privilege to extend
> the same for one two or three years,
> to the amount of $3000. The Lion is
> now in Philadelphia and is to be
> brought to this city. I am requested
> to ask if you will take the risk and at
> what premium? The Lion is

represented to be five years old and
in perfect health.

While the company universally declined to
insure the lives of animals, they began doing a
cautious business in slave risks. The Baltimore Life
was most likely the first life institution in the United
States to underwrite the lives of slaves. In fact, the
second policy ever issued by the company was for
$100 on the life of a slave named Jacob, and they
insured a handful of slaves almost every year during
the 1830s and 1840s. These risks accounted for
about 4% of the policies written by the Baltimore
Life through 1850. But the popularity of slave
policies – and the willingness of the Baltimore Life
to issue them – began increasing rapidly during the
1850s; by the eve of the Civil War, approximately
half of all policies sold by the company were on
slave risks. The vast majority of these slaves were
being insured through their Richmond agency,
which now dealt almost exclusively in slave
policies. Lucien Lewis, the company's new agent
in Richmond, stated on November 17, 1860 that he
did not even know what the company charged on
white lives but that "I do not anticipate doing much,
if anything, in that line."
The Civil War dealt a devastating blow to
the Baltimore Life. Unlike the majority of
companies based in the northern states, in the early
months of 1861 it was uncertain whether the
Baltimore Life's home state of Maryland eventually
would be a Union or Confederate state. A large
proportion of their policyholders resided in Virginia

and, since the mid-1850s, slave policies had formed an important segment of their business. In some cases, the unknown relationship between Maryland and the Confederacy strained policyholder allegiance. Dr. Thomas Pollard, medical examiner for the company in Richmond, complained on February 20, 1861: "Policy holders too in some instances have declined to renew insurance for fear of the position of Maryland in the Event of Virginias secession from the Union." But regardless of the ultimate fate of Maryland in the Union, the company remained sympathetic to the Confederacy and did not intend to differentiate between northern and southern war risks. By May 1861, the Baltimore Life was demonstrating their support of southern policyholders through their willingness to insure Confederate soldiers.

However, by the late spring and summer of 1861, this relationship between companies residing in Union states (including border states such as Maryland) and Confederate policyholders became much more difficult to maintain. In May, 1861, a Confederate act sequestered the debts of southerners owed to northerners. This law was extended in August when ownership of all property by northerners in the South was declared illegal and the Confederate government began to seize these assets, including bank deposits, stock and bond certificates, and debt contracts. On the Union side, mail service between the sections was halted by order of the United States Postmaster General in May, 1861. In July of that year, Congress declared several of the southern states to be in a condition of insurrection, which opened the door for President Abraham Lincoln to issue a presidential proclamation – commonly known as the Non-Intercourse Act – forbidding all commercial interaction between northern companies and southern states beginning on August 26, 1861. Meanwhile, Mississippi (and possibly other Confederate states) actively expelled northern life insurance companies from its borders, stating that the conditions necessary for renewing their licenses in that state were vitiated with the dissolution of the Union.

C. B. Wellford, the company's agent in Fredericksburg, VA, expressed his concern with underwriting new policies given the state of war in a letter dated October 25, 1861: "Communication with you is now so uncertain that it is useless to try to effect insurances unless some arrangement can be made by which risks can be made binding here. I merely submit the matter for your decision. . . . The tendency to the sequestration of property in your state has had its effects, but as far as I know, the confidence in your Co remains unshaken." Dr. Thomas Pollard, the Richmond medical examiner, similarly wrote to the company secretary F. M. Colston on December 14, 1861 and offered a temporary solution: "Parties are Enquiring [sic] of me what they shall do about paying premiums on their policies, and whether your Co. will hold themselves responsible for losses to be settled as soon as practicable. I suggest you authorize me to receive such premiums, and give such assurance. . . . The money I receive, might be appropriated to the payment of losses, or in such other way as you deem proper."

The Baltimore Life, with the most at stake in the South of any life insurance company, did everything in their power to bypass the obstacles for continuing their southern business. Responding to these letters, company president John I. Donaldson, and secretary F. M. Colston decided to cease writing new policies in the South and to authorize Dr. Pollard to collect premiums from existing policyholders in Richmond. Additionally, they instructed their agents in Fredericksburg, Petersburg, and Lynchburg, Virginia to remit premium payments from their agencies to Dr. Pollard, who would be responsible for paying all southern claimants during the war. Agents were also directed to accept payments offered in Confederate notes, "with the understanding that should a loss occur during the continuance of this State of affairs that the amount shall be paid in the same funds in which the premiums are now paid."

Despite these efforts, the physical and economic devastation of the war – including the emancipation of the slaves – placed the Baltimore Life in an extremely precarious financial condition. John I. Donaldson, who had served as president of the company since its incorporation in 1830, died on September 18, 1866, leaving his successor William G. Harrison with the difficult task of deciding the fate of the company. Before the end of that year, company executives were considering the feasibility of continuing to insure risks; they consulted with a highly respected actuary named

Sheppard Homans on several occasions regarding the valuation of their remaining policies and their future prospects for success. By February 1867, the Board of Directors and stockholders had determined that the best course of action would be to reinsure the remaining risks in another company. The company reached an agreement in May with the Equitable Life Assurance Society to obtain these risks, paying cash surrender values to any policyholders not wishing to have their policies transferred to New York. By the summer of 1867, the Baltimore Life Insurance Company had officially closed their doors.

Sharon Ann Murphy
Ph.D. Candidate
Corcoran Department of History
University of Virginia

Acknowledgements

The compilation of Genealogical data requires
the cooperation and assistance of many persons.
I am grateful for the assistance and
encouragement of all persons who assisted in
this work. The following persons gave
immeasurable assistance in this compilation:

Bill and Martha Reamy of the Maryland
Genealogical Society made me aware of the
existence of the source material at the Maryland
Historical Society.

Sharon Ann Murphy, University of Virginia
provided introductory and historical data used in
the appendixes.

Mary Herbert, Francis O'Neil, and Bea Hardy of
the Maryland Historical Society provided
assistance in locating materials, formatting data,
and continuous encouragement.

Sources

Baltimore Life Insurance Company Papers,
MS 175.
Manuscripts Department, Maryland
Historical Society.

Archives of Maryland, Electronic edition
Maryland State Archives, V. 153, Chap. 149

Baltimore Life Insurance Company Applications

Aaron, age 11: Born Dorchester Co., Md. Age about 26. Resides in Baltimore, Md. Slave employed as a hotel worker. Insured by John Hooper. 8 October 1849.

Abbett, Thomas M.: Born Philadelphia, Pa. 21 March 1806. Resides in Baltimore, Md. At # 27 Hollins St. Accountant. 1 December 1848.

Abercrombie, Mary F: Born 15 October 1796, Baltimore, Maryland. Resides in Baltimore, Maryland. (Charles St. near Franklin). 29 November 1836.

Adams, George: Born in Delaware, September 1800. Lieutenant, U. S. Navy. 11 March 1835.

Adams, Isaac, age 14; Thomas, age 8; James, age 6: Slaves Born in Baltimore, employed as house servants. Insured by William Gorsuch 9 April 1835.

Adams, William: Born in Delaware County, Pennsylvania 4 September 1806. Resides in Washington, D. C. Clerk in U. S. Treasury Department.

Addison, John C.: No data given insured by recommendation of C. W. Pairo, Washington, D. C.

Addison, John: Born 11 July 1810, Georgetown, District of Columbia 11 July 1810. Resides in Washington, D. c. Clerk in the General Land Office. 3 October 1836.

Albert, age 11, Born Richmond, house servant.

Aleck, 11: Born Nelson Co., Va. Slave, employed as a tobacco factory hand in Richmond, Va. Insured by Dr. R. T. Coleman

Alescandra: Born February 1825, Baltimore, Md. . Resides in Baltimore, Maryland. Slave insured by Nicholas Breeves 2 June 1834.

Alexander, John: Born 1798, Baltimore, Md. Master of the ship Elona Davidson en route to Wilmington, N. C; Goree, Africa & back to Baltimore. 20 December 1836.

Baltimore Life Insurance Company Applications

Alexander: Born in Baltimore, Maryland February 1825. Resides in Baltimore, Md. Slave employed as a waiter. Insured by Nicholas Brewer 2 June 1834.

Alfred, Joseph: Born Mecklenburg County, Virginia 18 November 1797. Resides in Baltimore, Maryland. Lawyer. 17 August 1834.

Allen, A. W: Born 22 February 1816, Davidson Co. Tenn.

Allen, James W: Born in Shelby County, Kentucky 17 March 1811. Resides in Shelby County, Kentucky. Practices Law in Henry County, Kentucky. 25 March 1841.

Allen, Thomas: Born 14 March 1811, near Elizabeth City, North Carolina. Resides in Elizabeth City, North Carolina. Merchant. 13 January 1841.

Allison, Henry: Born 23 December 1793, Stafford County, Virginia. Resides at Madison Court House, Virginia. Engaged in 'Commercial Pursuits'. 6 may 1834.

Amos, James E: Born Baltimore Co., Md. Resides in Baltimore, Md. City #82 Ensor St.. Born 1835. 11 October 1855.

Anderson, George W: Born Maryland. Age 34. Formerly resided in Baltimore, Md. Currently en route to California. Insured by David Feelmyer. 5 September 1851.

Anderson, John W: Born 3 February 1800, County Monaghan, Ireland. Resides in Louisville, Kentucky. Dry goods merchant. 10 June 1839.

Anderson, Richard: Born in Elk Ridge, Ann Arundel Co., Md. Age about 34. Resides in Baltimore, Md. A slave employed in a brickyard. Insured by Francis Burns 5 February 1833.

Anderson: Age about 19, employed on Richmond & Danville R.R. 7 January 1834. Mary R. Thornton, insurer.

Anderson: Born Va., age about 23. Residence in Virginia. Employed as an apothecary. Insured by W. W. Jones.

Baltimore Life Insurance Company Applications

Andrew, a slave: Born Henrico Co., Va. Age 15. Employed in tobacco Factory. Lives in Richmond, Va. Insured by Thomas W. Doswell, trustee for William P. H. Davenport.

Andrew: A slave of J. P. Winston of Richmond, Va. Insured 20 December 1855. Undated claim payment is noted.

Andrew: Born Henrico Co., Va. Age 12. Employed in tobacco factory. Lives in Richmond, Va. Insured by Thomas W. Doswell, trustee for William P. H. Davenport

Ann: Born in Missouri, age 13. Resides in St. Louis, Missouri. A slave employed as a house servant. Insured by William McNeal. 27 July 1849

Ann: Born Martinsburg, Va., 1838. Resides in Berkley County, Virginia. Servant. Insured by W. L. Compton 1 May 1841.

Anthony, 21: Born King William Co., Va. Residence Richmond, Va. Employed at Tobacco Factory. Slave insured by John J. Toler.

Armour, James: Born 14 October 1805, Baltimore, Maryland. Resides in Baltimore, Maryland. Merchant. July 1841.

Arthur, Robert: Born 22 July, 1819, Baltimore county, Maryland. Dentist, residing in Washington, D. C. 17 July 1852.

Athy, age 11: Born Middlesex, Va. J. P. Talley, Richmond, Va.

Atkinson, Joseph M.: Born 7 January 1820, Dinwiddie County, Virginia. Resides in Frederick city, Md. Pastor of Presbyterian Church. Sally Page Atkinson, spouse. 13 January 1851.

Austen, James H: Born 26 September 1788 in Baltimore, Maryland. 6 September 1831.

Austin, 15: Born King William Co., Va. Residence Richmond, Va. Employed at Tobacco Factory. Slave insured by John J. Toler.

Austin, Henry: Born 30 August 1817 in England. Resides in Prince George's Co., Md.

Baltimore Life Insurance Company Applications

Baden, John R: Born 12 May 1810, Prince George's Co., Maryland. Merchant, residing in Nottingham, Maryland. 13 May 1852.

Bailey, Thomas T.: Born 10 April 1799, Nelson County, Virginia. Resides in Henry County, Virginia. Currently farming, but intends to remove to Mississippi and engage in the Mercantile Business. 28 May 1835.

Baldwin, Daniel: B 24 April 1820, Baltimore, Md. Clerk at the Savings Bank of Baltimore,, residing in Baltimore, Md. 25 July 1853.

Baldwin, David: Born 24 April 1821, Baltimore, Maryland. Bank clerk at the Savings Bank of Baltimore, residing in Baltimore. 7 March 1853.

Baldwin, Frederick: Born 11 July 1794, Bridgeport, Fairfield county, Connecticut. Resides in Washington, D. C. Clerk at Post Office. 9 June 1835.

Ball, John L.: Born May 1806 in Virginia. Resides in Washington, D. C. Lieutenant in U. S. Navy. 12 July 1838.

Baltimore, Md. Resides in Baltimore, Md. Broker. 10 January 1846 and 9 February 1852.

Bankhead, Theophilis: Slave, employed as a boatman on the Chesapeake Bay. Insured by Samuel Philips, Fredericksburg, Virginia 13 August 1852.

Banks, George: Born Hanover, Va. Age 19. A slave hired out to work on the Danville Railroad. Insured by D. Lee Powell. 4 January 1834.

Barbour, Andrew: Born 15 February 1820, Washington, D. C. Resides in Georgetown, D. C. Married. Bricklayer. 18 February 1858.

Barnard, E. F: Born 3 August 1812, Boston, Massachusetts. Resides in Washington, D. C. Clerk in U. S. Navy Department. 2 January 1838.

Barnard, Edward: Born 21 February 1788, Massachusetts. Resides in Washington, D. C. Clerk in General Land Office of U. S. Treasury. 26 February 1833.

Barnes, Abraham: Born Maryland 1808. Residence near Georgetown. Clerk. 3 February 1851.

Baltimore Life Insurance Company Applications

Barnes, Frances Ida: Born 1810, Savannah, Ga. Mobile, Ala. Pasenger on Schooner Elvina. 28 December 1836.

Barnes, J. T. Mason: Born 4 April 1833, Maryland. Office clerk residing in Washington, D. C. 6 June 1853.

Barnes, William A.: Born in Baltimore, Md. 23 March 1809. Resides in Baltimore, Md. Going to California. Carpenter. Ellen E. Barnes, spouse. 9 April 1850.

Barney, John: Born in Baltimore, Maryland, 1785. Resides in Baltimore, Maryland. Merchant. 28 August 1835. Application indicates a spouse and daughter, both unnamed.

Barnum, Augustus: Born in Philadelphia, Pa. 24 February 1809. Resides in Greensboro Green, Alabama. Physician. 28 September 1849

Barnum, Theron: Born 28 April 1803 in Vermont. Resides in Baltimore, Maryland, traveling to Terre Haute, Indiana. Inn Keeper. 17 October 1838.

Barry, George W: Born 16 March 1813, Baltimore, Maryland. Resides in Washington, D. C. Clerk in the Register's Office of the U. S. Treasury Department. 16 January 1838. [1]

Barry, William R.: Born 28 June 1828, Baltimore, Maryland. Resides in Baltimore, Md. Hardware business at # 3 Hanover Street, Baltimore, Md. 18 March 1858.

Barton, Thomas B: Born 21 July 1849 in Baltimore, Md. Resides in Fredericksburg, Va. Lawyer. 21 July 1849.

Basley, Benjamin: Born 3 September 1821 in Mechanicsville, Pa. Resides in West Zanesville, Ohio. Carpenter. Insured by Robert M. Lee. 8 April 1850.

---

[1] Application also contains note denying death of one Thomas Ragsdale.

Baltimore Life Insurance Company Applications

Bass, Colin: Born 11 April 1807, Powhaten County, Virginia. Resides in Richmond, Virginia. Dry Goods employee. 23 April 1839.

Battee, Dennis H: Born 1786, Anne Arundel County, Maryland. Resides in Anne Arundel County, Maryland (West River). Farmer & Planter. Insured by Richard H. Battee of Baltimore, Maryland.

Baxter, Sydney S: Born Lexington, Va. 18 November 1802. Resides at Richmond, Va. Attorney General of the Sate of Virginia. 9 October 1838.

Beach, Miles: Born 20 October 1806 in Fairfield Co., Conn. Resides in St. Louis, Mo. A merchandiser, going to California. 27 March 1849.

Beall, Benjamin L: Born in Baltimore County, Maryland 31 October 1800. Resides in Washington, D. C. War Department clerk. 21 August 1833.

Beam, Robert M: Born 15 July 1803, Baltimore County, Maryland. Resides in Baltimore, Maryland. Innkeeper, Globe Hotel, Baltimore, Maryland. 12 November 1840.

Beers, Isaac: Born in Stratford, Connecticut 4 June 1794. Resides in Washington, D. C. Pawn broker.8 December 1835.

Bell, George B: Born 22 September 1839, Stanford, Kentucky. Resides in Louisville, Kentucky. In the Grocery business. 25 March 1839.

Bell, John W.: Born 10 January 1822 in New York, N. Y. Residence in Baltimore, Md. Commission Merchant. 7 October 1851.

Belt, Thomas H: Born 1789, Baltimore Co. Elizabeth K. Belt, wife, born Cecil Co. 23 May 1798. 8 November 1831.

Benjamin, 18: Born Hanover Co., Va. Employed in brickyard. Insured by Thomas Pollard for John Henry Wickham.

Bennett, Henry: Born Baltimore about 28 years ago.8 October 1831.

Bentz, Samuel: Born 26 September 1802 in Washington Co., Md. Resides in Boonsboro, Md. Farmer. 21 January 1850.

Baltimore Life Insurance Company Applications

Bernard, Overton: Born in Flovenna, Virginia 2 April 1798. Resides in Portsmouth, Virginia. Merchandiser. 17 August 1838.

Berry, Brook M.: Born in the District of Columbia, January 1794. A clerk in the office of the Clerk of the U. S. House of Representatives. 27 February 1834.

Berryman, A. H.: Born Port Royal, Va. 10 October 1812. Resides in Washington, D. C. U. S. Navy. 24 March 1838.

Berryman, O. H. 44: Born Virginia 10 October 1812. U. S. Navy Captain. 23 May 1856.

Betts, Royston: Born 25 February 1814, Northumberland County, Virginia. Resides in Baltimore, Maryland. 11 February 1842.

Beverly: A slave owned by B. L. Winston, Richmond, Va. Insured for $ 500.

Beverly: Born 1844 Buckingham County, Va. laborer on Va. & Tenn. RR

Beylen/Baylor: Born 1835 in Caroline Co., Va. Residence in Richmond, Va. Driver & carpenter. Slave, insured by Dr. R. T. Coleman.

Bibb, George W: Born in Prince Edward County, Virginia 30 October 1776. Resides in Louisville, Kentucky. Chancellor of the Louisville Chancery Court. 26 September 1842.

Bickley, Samuel: Born 14 August 1792, Ellesmere, Shropshire, England. Resides in Baltimore, Maryland. 23 May 1837.

Billing, William W. Born 16 August 1801, Washington, D. C. Resides in Washington, D. C. Clerk in U. S. War Department. 6 March 1838.

Billop, Grundy T: Merchant Born and residing in Baltimore, Maryland. Date of Birth is 1820. 7 October 1852.

Bird, Permanes: Born in King & Queen County, Virginia, June 1790. Resides in Plymouth, King & Queen County, Virginia. Farmer & Commissioner of Revenue. 7 February 1835.

Baltimore Life Insurance Company Applications

Bishop, William F: Born 29 August 1809, Baltimore, Md. Resides in Louisville, Kentucky. Tobacco merchant. 17 December 1836.

Bissouard, Thomas Joseph: Born Paris, France 24 March 1787.

Bixler, Daniel: Born Baltimore, Maryland. Tobacco manufacturer. Traveling to West Virginia, New Orleans, La. 15 November 1838.

Blackburne, Anna Eliza: Born May 1816, Philadelphia, Pa. Resides in Phiadelphia, Pa. Wife of Francis Blackburne, merchant. 19 January 1837.

Blackford, William B: Born 19 August 1801, Frederick Co., Md. Resides at Fredericksburg, Virginia. Newspaper editor. 23 March 1839.

Blaine, Archibald M: Born 28 February 1816, Barren County, Kentucky. Resides in Louisville, Kentucky. Dry goods merchant. 15 January 1836.

Blair, Joseph H: Born 2 August 1827 in Indiana. Resides in Monticello Missouri. Going to California. 30 March 1849.

Blake, John A: Born 28 May 1800, Grafton County, New Hampshire. Resides in Washington, D. C. Bookbinder. 9 October 1841.

Blakistone, James T: Clerk of the Circuit Court of St. Mary's County, Maryland. Born and resides in St. Mary's County, Maryland. Born 26 February 1815.

Boardley, James (colored): Age 29. Resides in Baltimore, Md. Insured by and lives with John M. Smith. 21 November 1849.

Boggs, Alexander L: Born 13 October 1792, Lancaster County, Pennsylvania. Resides in Baltimore, Md. Merchant. 2 July 1834.

Bond, Thomas: Born in Washington D. C. 15 August 1800. Resides in Port Deposit, Maryland. Merchant. 21 September 1836.

Bond, William: Born Annapolis, Md, 3 January 1804. Resides in Baltimore, Md. Occupation pyrotechnic Ian. 3 April 1857.

Baltimore Life Insurance Company Applications

Bone, James: Born 25 June 1835 in New York State. Resides in Ellicott City, Md. Storekeeper. 20 January 1856. .

Boon, Jim Ruffin: Born New Kent Co, Va.. Slave employed as a coal pit hand in Henrico Co, Va., married.William R. Trent Insurer.

Booth, Junius Brutus: Born 1 May 1796, London England. Resides in Harford County, Maryland. Dramatic Performer. 15 January 1838.

Bordley, John: Born on the Eastern shore of Maryland. Age 49. Resides in Baltimore, Md. Portrait Painter. Insured by Francis P. Bordley. 14 May 1849.

Bosley, John H: Born 12 January 1811 in Baltimore, Md. Resides in Baltimore, Md. Unemployed. Coverage denied for trip to California. 26 July 1850

Boston, Charles: A slave belonging to Camilla M. Pollard of Richmond, Va. Insured 12 June 1834 and 28 February 1857. Undated notation of paid claim.

Boswell, Thomas H.: Born in Petersburg, Virginia. Age between 36 and 36. Resides in Fauquier County, Virginia. Farmer. Insured by John J. Royall. 19 July 1838.

Bowdre, Lucian A: Born Cumberland County, Georgia, 1811/12. Resides in Russell County, Alabama. Plantation manager. Insured by Augustine Leftwich 21 May 1839.

Bowie, Robert: Born 4 April 1804, Prince George's County, Maryland. Resides in Prince George's County, Md. Planter. 22 December 1837.

Bradford, John S.: Born 19 February 1820, Baltimore, Maryland. Resides in Washington, D. C. Broker.

Bradley, William A: Born 25 February 1794, Litchfield, Conn. Resides in Washington, D. C. Waiter. 30 April 1841.

Branch, David Mann: Born in Buckingham, Virginia 22 July 1809. Resides in Richmond, Virginia. Tobacconist, Branch & Cowles Tobacco. 3 July 1835.

Baltimore Life Insurance Company Applications

Branda, Augustus: Born 4 April 1795, L'Orient, France. Merchant, residing in Norfolk, Virginia. March 1841.

Brannan, Elizabeth: Born May 1827 in Maine. Resides in Baltimore, Md. Spouse Robert Brannan. 12 April 1850.

Brecht, Charles: Born 12 September 1801, Luchow, Hanover, Germany. Resides in Baltimore, Maryland. Silk business. Has mother, one brother, and five sisters residing in Europe. 8 April 1841.

Breckinridge, Francis C: Born 24 August 1806, New Orleans, Louisiana. Resides in Louisville, Kentucky. Presbyterian Minister. Previous residences in Princeton, New Jersey and Lexington, Kentucky. 19 February 1836.

Brewer, John M: Lawyer. Born September 1822, Annapolis, Maryland. Resides in Cumberland, Maryland. 23 February 1853.

Brocchus, Perry E.: Born In Virginia, 1816. Residence in Washington D. C., Lawyer. Letter attached to application indicates that the insured plans to travel to Salt Lake City Utah. 4 November 1850.

Bronaugh, John W: 5 May 1857. Age 43, Born Georgetown, D. C. 11 August 1804. Resides in Georgetown. Employed as office clerk.

Brooke, Walter T.: Born 17 September 1802, Fairfax County, Virginia. Resides in Washington, D. C. Clerk in General Land Office. 10 December 1833.

Brooks, Alexander: Born 5 May 1815, Chesterfield, Virginia. Resides Gerrito, Powhatten County, Virginia. Country Store Keeper. 1838.

Brooks, John: Born Prince George's Co., Md. 28 August 1787. Residence in Prince George's Co. " near Marlborough Plantation. Farmer. 11 December 1850.

Broom, Frances Virgilia: Born 12 May 1834, Washington, D. C. Resides with her parents in Washington, D. C. Insured by Jacob Broom 28 October 1835.

Baltimore Life Insurance Company Applications

Broom, Jacob: Born 25 July 1808, Baltimore, Md. Resides in Washington, D. C. Lawyer & clerk in General post office. 3 September 1834.

Broomwell (Broomwill ?), W. J: Born Sussex Co., Va. 9 March 1808. Application date 5 September 1855.

Brotherton, Thomas W: Mariner, Born 6 January 1794, Baltimore, Maryland. Resides in Baltimore, Maryland. 22 February 1849.

Brown, Alfred James: Dental Surgeon Born in Baltimore, Maryland 1823. Resides in Baltimore. 5 February 1853.

Brown, Charles B: Born in Newark, New Jersey 27 May 1804. Resides in Washington, D. C. Postal clerk. 5 June 1834.

Brown, Edmund F: Born 27 February 1807, Newark, New Jersey. Resides at Washington, D. C. Post Office Clerk. 3 March 1834.

Brown, Elijah: Negro "formerly the property of Mrs. R. Cromwell. Employed as Ostler in stable. Insured 27 November 1837. Insured by Nicholas L. Wood 27 November 1837.

Brown, George W: Born Shepherdstown, Virginia. Resides at Harper's Ferry, Virginia. Military Store Keeper's Clerk at U. S. Armory. 20 January 1837.

Brown, Harriet: Age about 15. No other data give. A slave insured by Solomon Corner, owner. 20 September 1851.

Brown, J. W.: Born March 1798, North Carolina. Resides in Washington, D. C. Office clerk. 10 February 1852.

Bryan, Joseph: Born 1813 in Tennessee. Planter, residing in North Mississippi.

Buchanan, Franklin: B 7 September 1801, Baltimore, Maryland. U. S. Navy Commander, residing on the eastern shore of Maryland. 3 March 1847.

Buchinal, James: Born 4 March 1799, Q. A. Co. Residence Baltimore, tailor. 22 September 1831.

Baltimore Life Insurance Company Applications

Buddy, John: Born in Pennsylvania. Age 47. Resides in Baltimore, Maryland. 17 November 1840.

Bullock, Erasmus: Born in Orange County, North Carolina, August 1807. Resides in Georgetown, District of Columbia. U. S. War Department Clerk. 2 October 1835.

Burchard, Matthew H: Born 30 June 1815 in Lake Co., Ohio. Resides in Greenville, Ill. Going to California. 7 March 1849.

Burke, James M: Born 16 March 1815, Richmond, Virginia. Resides at Washington, D. C. Works in office of the Comptroller of the Treasury. 7 January 1839.

Busk, Harriet Josephine: Born 24 November 1804, Baltimore, Maryland. Resides at Baltimore, Maryland. Housewife. 26 September 1837.

Bustun, John B: Born Chesterfield Co., Virginia 16 September 1849. Resides in Baltimore, Maryland. Clerk. 13 June 1849.

Butler, Jeff age 8: house servant, Richmond, Virginia. Born Washington , D.C. James Mander, applicant, 6 April 1834.

Butler, John O: Born Caroline Co., Va. 6 December 1820. Married, farmer & surveyor, residence Caroline Co. Va. 5 May 1856.

Cain, Gustavius: Born October 1826, Fauquier County, Virginia. Laborer, residing in Fauquier County, Va. 19 March 1853.

Camp, John G: Born1789, Virginia. Resides in Tallahassee, Florida. Marshall. 25 September 1841.

Campbell, Bernard U. /W: Born February 1796, Frederick Co. Md. residence Baltimore teller @ Merchants Bank.18 January 1832

Carey, John L.: Born 1812 in Sussex Co., Delaware. Residence in Baltimore, Md. Newspaper Editor. 8 September 1849.

Cargill, Elbert: Born in New York 4 January 1816. Resides in Zanesville, Ohio. Spouse is Mary Ann Cargill. Cooper.

Baltimore Life Insurance Company Applications

Carmichael, Edward H. Dr: Insured by John James Chew 28 February 1848.

Carmichael, Edward H.: Born Fredericksburg, Va. 2 August 1796. Residence in Richmond, Va., physician 22 February 1848. Insured by Charles C. Willford.

Carmichael, Edward H: Born 2 August 1796, Fredericksburg, Virginia. Resides in Fredericksburg. Physician. 27 June 1833.

Carmichael, James: Born 14 March 1835, Fredericksburg, Virginia. Resides in Fredericksburg, Va. Editor. 1 April 1858.

Carothers, Andrew: Born in Pennsylvania 29 February 1803. Resides in Washington, D. C. 29 July 1849.

Carothers, Peter: Born in Scotland. Age 34. Resides in Baltimore, Md. Carpenter. Going to California.

Carpenter, William H: Born London, England, 1814. Resides "6 miles on the Frederick Road", Baltimore County, Md. Farmer. Insured by John Fowler 21 June 1842.

Carr, Dabney L.: Born Albemarle county, Virginia. Resides in Baltimore County, Maryland. Naval Officer for the Port of Baltimore. 23 September 1834.

Carr, Dabney S: Born at Albemarle County, Virginia 11 March 1802. Resides in Baltimore County, Maryland between the Harford & York Turnpikes. Naval Officer. 22 February 1839.

Carr, Overton: Born in Maryland 1782. Resides in Washington, D. C. Doorkeeper of the U. S. House of Representatives. 8 August 1832.

Carr, William: Born 1810, District of Columbia. Resides in Washington, D. C. Clerk in the Office of the Secretary of the U. S. Senate. 5 April 1838.

Carr: F. W: Born March 1800, New Hampshire. Resides at Deep Creek, Virginia. Merchant. 14 November 1837.

Carroll, Henrietta M: Born in Baltimore, Md. In 1790. Housewife. 3 April 1854.

Baltimore Life Insurance Company Applications

Carson, Joshua: Born Baltimore, Md. 27 January 1822. Resides in Baltimore, Maryland on Josephine Street. Carpenter.

Carter, Elizabeth O: Born December 1796 at Belmont, Loudon County, Virginia. Resides at Oatland, Loudon County, Virginia. Housewife. Insured by Catherine Powell   12 December 1837.

Carter, George: Slave insured by John T. Councilman.21 January 1851. Born Anne Arundel County, Md. 19 June 1830. Residence & is employed as a farmhand near Pikesville, Md.

Carter, Mary Randolph: Born Strafford Co., Va. 19 October 1780. Resides in Fredericksburg, Va. Housekeeper 22 January 1850.

Carter, Robert: Born in Maine, July 1786. Resides in Baltimore, Maryland Merchantile business. 22 June 1834.

Causon, John M: Born in St. Mary's County, Maryland 1 February 1810. Resides at St. Mary's County. Attorney at Law. Insured by Benjamin Gantt. 2 February 1839.

Chalmers, Charles: Born 5 April 1813 in Baltimore, Maryland. Resides in Washington, D. C. Lieutenant in the U. S. Artillery. 17 October 1835.

Chamberlagne: Born King William Co., Va. Residence Richmond, Va. Employed at Tobacco Factory. Slave insured by John J. Toler.

Chamberlain, Edward: Born Baltimore, Md. December 1825. Resides in Baltimore, Md. Bricklayer. 21 May 1850.

Chambers, John J. Born Mercersburg, Pennsylvania 22 September 1824. Resides in Mercersburg, Pa. Farmer.

Chappell, Philip L: Born 26 November 1800, Baltimore County, Maryland. Resides in Baltimore, Maryland. Druggist. 1 January 1835.

Baltimore Life Insurance Company Applications

Charity, 40: Born Maryland, 1817. Residence Washington, D. C., House Servant. Owner S. A. Elliot purchased from William Dangerfield. 17 June 1856.

Charles, 16: Born Hanover, Va. Resides in Richmond, Va. Slave employed in brick making. Insured by William O. Winston for the benefit of Mrs. E. Christian & children, owners.

Charles, a slave: Born Richmond, Va. Employed and residence in Richmond, Va. Insured by R. L. Winston.

Chew, Henry M: Farmer, Born in Anne Arundel County Maryland 17 March 1801. Resides in Nottingham, Maryland. 9 May 1848.

Chew, John James: Born Frederick, Virginia 2 July 1835. Resides in Frederick, Va. Court Clerk, Lawyer. 2 July 1835.

Chew, John James: Born in Fredericksburg, Va. 20 July 1803. Resides in Fredericksburg, Va. Court Clerk. 12 July 1857.

Chew, Thomas I (J ?): 27 November 1848. Born Calvert Co. 25 October 1811. Occupation planter. Resides Chestnut Hill, Prince Georges Co, Md.[2]

Cicero, 16: Born Nelson Co., Va. Residence in Richmond, Va. Employed as tobacco factory hand. Slave. Insured by Dr. R. T. Coleman.

Clare, Thomas I.: Born 8 November 1810, Calvert County, Maryland. Resides in Baltimore, Maryland. Clerk to Asa Needham. 14 January 1835.

Clark, James H: Insuring **Betty**, a slave Born in Gates County, North Carolina sometime before 1800, employed as a cook; **Martha, daughter of Betty**, Born in Portsmouth, Virginia March 1834; **Henry**, a slave Born in Gates County, North Carolina 24 December 1828, employed as a house servant. October, 1835.

---

[2] Application contains note from Samuel Chew, physician attesting to the good health of the applicant.dated 11 April 1857.

Baltimore Life Insurance Company Applications

Clark, John: Born 20 August 1797, Annapolis, Maryland. Resides in Baltimore, Maryland. Lottery Agent. Insured by third party, name illegible. 10 February 1837.

Clark, Shelby, 28; Born Prince George's Co., Md. Resides Upper Marlboro, Md. Attorney. 25 November 1856

Clarke, Merriwether Lewis: Born St. Louis Missouri 10 January 1809. Resides in St. Louis, Missouri. U.S. Surveyor General for Illinois and Missouri. 16 May 1850. Insured by Thomas M. Abbot, Mutual Life Insurance Co.

Clarke, Robert P.: Born in Canon's burgh, Washington County, Pennsylvania 11 October 1802. resides in Wheeling, Va. Steamboat master on the Ohio & Mississippi rivers. 12 September 1834.

Clarke, W. B: Born Georgetown, District of Columbia 4 September 1817. Resides in Hagerstown, Maryland. Lawyer. 30 May 1850.

Claxton, Alexander:, Born Philadelphia, Pa. Jan. 1793. Naval Officer, residence, Baltimore. 4 November 1831.

Clay, 12: Born Chesterfield, Va. Slave, employed at Black Heath Coal Pits. Insured by Theodore Tompkins for William E. Martin.

Claybrook, George: Age about 38. Traveling to California. 30 May 1853.

Claybrooke, George: En route to California, insured by his brother in law, W. H. Dorsey.

Clemens, Augustus D: Born 22 July 1818, Baltimore, Md. Resides at Beach Hill, West Saratoga St, Baltimore, Md. Law student. Beneficiary is Henrietta U. Clemans.

Clements, Bennett: Born 23 March 1789, Maryland. Resides in Georgetown, District of Columbia. Treasury Department clerk. 12 April 1838.

Clements, Charles B: Born in Georgetown, District of Columbia September 1820. Resides in Georgetown. Is planning to relocate to Missouri. Teacher. 5 May 1842.

16

Baltimore Life Insurance Company Applications

Clements, William: Born Georgetown, District of Columbia September 1824. Resides in the Southwest Territory, U. S. A. Paymaster's Clerk, U. S. Army. Insured by Bernard Clements, Georgetown, D. C. 7 September 1846.

Clendenine, Dr. Alexander: Born 8 July 1791, York District of South Carolina. Resides in Baltimore, Maryland. Physician. On an extended trip to the Southern and western states of the U. S. Insured by his wife Mary Louisa Clendenin 25 April 1842.

Clendenine, Jane: Born Baltimore, Maryland 20 April 1804. Resides in Baltimore, Maryland. Insured by George Rosenstock.

Coakley, Phillip H: Born 28 December 1800, King George County, Virginia. Broker, residing in Baltimore, Maryland. 25 June 1853.

Coburn, Thomas J. Born in Kentucky 20 May 1818. Resides in St. Louis, Missouri. Clerk. Going to California.

Cockey, Edward: Born 11 May 1805, Baltimore County, Maryland. Resides in Baltimore, Maryland (92 North Howard Street). Lime & Feed Store owner. 9 November 1835.

Cockey, Joshua: Born in Frederick Co., Md. 5 September 1801. Resides in Baltimore, Maryland. Employed in the City of Baltimore Records Office.

Cohen, David I: Born 30 April 1800, Richmond, Va. Resides in Baltimore, Maryland. 25 September 1837.

Cole, Jane. Born Queen Anne's Co., Md. 1833. A slave residing at 32 Franklin Street, Baltimore, Md. Employed as a house servant by W. Dennings. Insured by William Easter of Hartford Co., Md.

Coleman, John: Born 1822 Hanover County, Va. Resides Franklin County, Va. laborer at Va. & Tenn. RR.

Coles, William jr: Born 16 February 1812, Somerset Shire, England. Resides in Baltimore, Maryland. Shoemaker. Sailing for England. 17 May 1839.

Baltimore Life Insurance Company Applications

Collins, David C.: Born 3 February 1805, Middletown, Connecticut. Resides in Middletown, Connecticut. Treasurer, Collins Manufacturing Co. 11 June 1835.

Collins, John A: Born in Delaware 11 February 1801. Resides in Baltimore, Maryland. M. E. minister. 1 October 1849.

Collins, Joseph S: Born Sussex County, Delaware 17 March 1799. Resides in Georgetown, District of Columbia. Clerk in the General Land Office. 11 July 1834.

Collins, Samuel W.: .: Born 8 September 1802, Middletown, Connecticut. Resides in Middletown, Connecticut. Superintendent of an Axe Factory. 11 June 1835.

Connell, John: Born 23 February 1784. Resides in Philadelphia, Pennsylvania. 25 February 1834.

Conway, Eustace: Born 19 September 1820 in Stafford, Virginia. Lawyer. 25 October 1849.

Cook, Charles: Born Ohio in 1824. Railroad Conductor. Residence in Baltimore, Md. 13 November 1855.

Cooke, Edward E: Born 5 October 1792, Alexandria, District of Columbia. Resides in Charlestown, Jefferson County, Virginia. Attorney at Law. 3 May 1839.

Coolee, John D: Born in Bermuda or Sommers Islands 17 June 1787. Resides in Frederick County, Virginia. Lawyer. 31 November 1836.

Coolidge, James: Born in Upper Marlborough, Prince George's County, Maryland 18 June 1805. Resides in Washington, D. C. Clerk in the General Post Office. 22 August 1836.

Cooper, Erwin I: Born 19 September 1820 in Philadelphia, Pennsylvania. Resides in Baltimore, Maryland. Lime burner. 7 April 1849.

Cooper, John /Jacob: Born 22 January 1830 In Baltimore County, Maryland. Resides in Ohio. Going to California. Farmer. 9 March 1850.

Baltimore Life Insurance Company Applications

Cooper, Samuel: Born 1 January 1816, Boston, Massachusetts. Resides in Louisville, Kentucky. Merchant. 30 October 1837.

Cooper, William B: Born in Maryland 18 July 1805. Resides in Baltimore, Maryland Spouse is Louise Cooper. Steam Saw Mill employee. 1 April 1850.

Couldson, William: Sandpaper manufacturer, Born in Boston, Massachusetts, residing in Baltimore, Maryland on Lexington Street. 17 September 1852.

Cox, John P. (colored): Post and rail maker Born and residing in Frederick County, Maryland 20 July 1825. 12 October 1852.

Crabb, Horatio N: Born Middletown, Pennsylvania. Resides in Washington, D. C. Assistant Clerk, U. S. House of Representatives. 14 August 1838.

Cragg, Jonathan W.: Born 8 May 1810, England. Resides in Baltimore. Sailing to Kingston, Jamaica; and Havana, Cuba on the Brig Angola. 14 March 1834.

Cranch, William: Born 17 July 1769 at Weymouth, Massachusetts. Resides in Washington, D. C. Cief Judge of the District of Columbia. 22 August 1836.

Creacy, James: Born 29 December 1789, Chowan County, North Carolina. Clerk, residing in Washington, D. C. 19 January 1853.

Creery, Joshua J.: Born 19 October 1826 in Baltimore, Maryland. Resides in Baltimore, Maryland. Clerk.

Cronise, Jacob: Born in Frederick county, Maryland 6 December 1830. Resides in Frederick county, Maryland. Teacher. Application date is illegible.

Cross, Dennis B: Born in Prince George's County, Maryland 3 January 1803. Resides in Washington, D. C. Book Keeper. 7 December 1835.

Crouch, Sam, about 40: Birthplace unknown. Employed at Allen & Preston Tobacco Factory, Richmond, Va., married, a slave. Insured by William Winston Jones.

Crouch, Sam, app. 40: Birthplace unknown. Employed at Allen & Preston Tobacco Factory,

Baltimore Life Insurance Company Applications

Richmond, Va., married , a slave. Insured by William Winston Jones.

Crummer, Edward A: Born 7 October 1807, Carlisle, Pennsylvania. Resides in Baltimore, Maryland. Bricklayer.28 December 1835.

Culbertson, Louis: Born 13 October 1817 in Muskingum County, Ohio. Resides in Falls Township, Ohio. Farmer. Insured by Thomas Bell. 9 April 1850.

Currier, Nathaniel: Born 14 January 1798 in Portsmouth, New Hampshire. Resides in Norfolk, Virginia. 2 February 1850.

Curtis, William: Born 4 November 1827 in Wayne Township, Ohio. Resides in Duncan Falls, Ohio. Insured by Stephen D. Carnes. Tailor.

Cutts, James M: Born 29 July 1805, Saco, Maine. Resides in Washington, D. C. Clerk in U. S. Treasury Department. 6 September 1839.

Dabney, 16: Born Hanover Co. Va. Resides in Richmond, Va. Employed in brickyard. Insured by Thomas Pollard for John Henry Wickham.

Dana, Matilda W.: Born in Cambridge, Massachusetts 1796. Resides in Georgetown, D. C. An instructress (teacher). December, 1835.

Danacott, John: 6 February 1834 insures **Duby Johnson,** Born in Hanover County, age 23, resides in Dinwiddie County, employed at coal mine of Mr. Hall. **Mary,** age 24, resides in Richmond, washer woman.

Daniel, 40-42: Born Henrico Co. Resides in Richmond, Va. Married. Employed in a Tannery. Not dated.

Daniel, age 30: Born Hanover County, Va. Works on Danville R. R. insured by Benjamin Pollard.

Daphney: Born Hanover Co., Va. Residence: Henrico Co., Va.

Dashiell, Mary: Born in Dorchester County, Maryland, 1807. Resides in Baltimore, Maryland. Has resided in Dorchester, County, Maryland. Housewife. Spouse is William C. N. 20 May 1836.

Baltimore Life Insurance Company Applications

Dashiell, William & Mary: Insured by Thomas Byrn, Dorchester County, Maryland 31 January 1838.
Dashiell, William C. N: Born in Somerset County, Maryland, 1807. Resides in Baltimore, Maryland. Has resided in Dorchester, County, Maryland. Mercantile business. Spouse is Mary. 20 May 1836.
David: Born in 1814 in Virginia. Resides in St. Louis, Missouri. A slave employed as a drayman. 28 May 1849.
Davis, John A.: Born in Franklin County, North Carolina. Resides in Maryland. Lieutenant, U. S. Navy 2 July 1835.
Davis, John A.: Born in Littlestown, Pennsylvania 10 July 1808. Resides in Emmitsburg, Maryland. Going to California. 22 April 1849.
Davis, William Frederick: Born 4 July 1817, Petersburg, Virginia. Resides in Petersburg, Virginia. Accountant at Petersburg Branch of the Bank of Virginia. 26 June 1839.
Davis, William Jr.: Born 1804, New York City. Resides in Washington, D. C. Land Office Clerk. 26 January 1837.
Davy: A slave owned by George Whitlock, Richmond, Va. Insured for $800. Claim paid 9 July 1858.
Davy: Age about 43. Slave of George Whitlock. Carpenter, residing in Richmond, Va.
Deal, Jannette: Born in Baltimore, Maryland. Age 31. Resides in Friendship, Anne Arundel County, Maryland. Spouse is Rev. William G. Deal. Insured by Robert Perry. 21 January 1841.
Dean, William. Insured 7 November 1850. Spouse and beneficiary Mary A. Dean.
Dean, William: Born Alexandria, D. C. 31October 1801. Residence in Alexandria, D. C. Plans to travel west. Beneficiary: Mary A. Dean & his heirs. 13 November 1843.
Deas, Charles: Born Charleston, S. C., age 27. Resides in Charleston, S.C., Naval Officer. Insured by Joshua W. Hall. 1 April 1847.

Baltimore Life Insurance Company Applications

DeHaven, Edwin J: Born in Philadelphia, Pensylvania 1816. Lieutenant U. S. Navy. 4 October 1842.

Denson, James H.: Born 26 September 1806 in Somerset County, Maryland. Resides in Baltimore, Maryland. Deputy Sheriff. 26 March 1849.

Detrick, Eddington: Born in Frederick county, Maryland 30 April 1839. Resides in Frederick County, Maryland. Mercantile Merchant. 1 May 1850.

Diana: Born Hanover Co.,Va. , age about 28, residence Richmond, Va. Slave. Owner John Daracott.

Dick, 16: Hanover County, Va. resides in Richmond, house servant. Richard F. Danacott.

Dick, a slave: Born Hanover County, Va., age 20. Employed on Danville R.R.

Dick, a slave: Born Henrico Co., Va. Age 12. Employed in tobacco Factory. Lives in Richmond, Va. Insured by Thomas W. Doswell, trustee for William P H. Davenprout.

Dickey, George A: Born September 1798 at Dauphin County, Pennsylvania. Resides in Baltimore, Maryland. Merchant. 19 March 1837.

Dickey, Miles W: Born in Bourbon county, Kentucky. 28 January 1801. Resides in Scott County, Kentucky. Farmer. 19 November 1835.

Dielman, Henry: Born in Frankford, Germany 26 April 1811. Resides in Washington, D. C. Music instructor. 28 July 1838.

Dite, 40:, resides in Henrico County. 6 January 1834. Benjamin Pollard.

Doane, George W.: Burlington, N. J. Bishop of Diocese of New Jersey, to insure Eliza Green Doane.6 March 1839.

Dohn, Franklin: Born 25 July 1814 , Baltimore, Maryland. Resides in Baltimore, Maryland. House carpenter. 9 October 1850.

Baltimore Life Insurance Company Applications

Donaldson, Dr. Frank: Born. 22 July 1823 in Baltimore, Md. Resides in Baltimore. A physician. Application Date 21 July 1835.

Dorsey, Benjamin H: Born in Anne Arundel Co., Md. Age 28. Resides in Baltimore, Md. Clerk. 25 November 1836.

Dorsey, John L: Born 14 December 1803, Charles county, Maryland. Resides in St. Mary's County, Maryland. 8 January 1852.

Dorsey, Lorenzo: Born 19 October 1808, Baltimore, Maryland. Bank Clerk. 1 December 1838.

Dorsey, Vernon J.: Born November 1826 in Maryland. Resides in Baltimore, Maryland. Going to California. 31 January 1849

Dougherty, William: Born in Bladensburg, Maryland 8 March 1802. Resides in Washington, D. C. Mercantile business. 19 May 1835.

Douglass, Jacob: Born in Ireland 1788. Came to America in 1798. Resides at Fauquier County, Virgina. Farmer. 8 February 1839.

Dow, Jesse E: Born Windham Co., Conn. 21 January 1809. Clerk in General Post Office, Washington, D. C. 26 August 1837.

Drew, Thomas H: Born May 1785 in Cumberland County, Virginia. Resides in Richmond, Virginia. Grocery manager.13 August 1838.

Dryden, Joshua: Born September 1792, Worcester County, Maryland. Resides at # 80 Liberty Street, Baltimore, Maryland. Taylor & Brick maker. 2 February 1841.

DuBarry, Edmund: Born at Philadelphia, Pennsylvania 4 July 1797. Family resides at Washington, D. C. Insured is U. S. Naval Surgeon, assigned to the U. S. Steamer Fulton. 25 February 1839.

Duffield, John Martin: Born 26 October 1812, Snow Hill, Maryland. Resides in Washington, D. C. Treasury Department clerk. 6 August 1834.

Baltimore Life Insurance Company Applications

Duke, Nathaniel: Born in Calvert County, Maryland 2 April 1799. Resides in Calvert County, Maryland. Farmer. 13 November 1848.

Dulany, William Captain: Letter attesting to the good health of Captain Dulany from U. S. Naval Surgeon, Signature illegible.

Duncan, Joseph M: Born Philadelphia, Pennsylvania 7 September 1801. Resides at Washington, D. C. Clerk at the U. S. Department of State. 28 November 1832.

Dungan, Abel S.: Born in Baltimore Maryland 15 November 1819. Residence is Baltimore, Maryland. Merchandiser. 1 February 1849.

Dunning, Joseph L.: Born in Washington County, Pennsylvania. Resides in Zanesville, Ohio. Saddler. Insured by Austin K. Hall. 11 April 1850.

Durkee, Pearl: Born 23 March 1805. Resides in Baltimore, Maryland. Cabinet Maker. 1 October 1836.

Durkee, Stephen S. K.: Born in Baltimore, Maryland 6 August 1807. Resides in Baltimore, Maryland. Cabinet maker. 3 April 1832.

Duryee, C. H: Born in New York, New York 7 August 1805.

Eagleston, Rebecca: Born in Baltimore, Maryland. Age 55. Resides in Baltimore, Maryland. Householder. 15 July 1836.

Early, Eleazer: Born 1 May 1781, Culpeper, Virginia. (Now Madison Co., Va.) Resides in Washington D. C. Clerk, U. S. House of Representatives. 24 December 1833.

Eaton, Nathan: Born 14 July 1790 in Massachusetts. Resides in Washington, D. C. works in U. S. Navy department. 8 December 1835.

Eaton, Nathaniel: Born 28 June 1807, Massachusetts. Resides in Washington, D. C. U. S. Army. 8 December 1835.

Edes, Richard A.: Born in Baltimore, Maryland in 1825. Resides in Baltimore, Maryland. Merchant. 6 June 1850.

Baltimore Life Insurance Company Applications

Edmond, Robert: Born 27 March 1808, Vergennes, Vermont. Resides in Richmond, Virginia. Mail contractor for E. C. Porter & Co. 6 February 1836.

Edmond. A slave of William C. Winston, Hanover Co., Va. Insured 28 February 1857.

Edward, 22: Born Chesterfield, Va. Slave, employed at Black Heath Coal Pits. Insured by Theodore Tompkins for William E. Martin.

Edward, 27: Born Hanover Co., Va. Employed in Iron Foundry. Slave insured by Henry Wickham 15 December 1856.

Edward, 27: Born Hanover Co., Va. Employed in Iron Foundry. Slave insured by Henry Wickham 15 December 1856.

Eliza: Born in Virginia. Age 13. Resides in St. Louis, Missouri. A slave employed as a house servant. Insured by Ferdinand M. Stevenson. 11 June 1849.

Eliza: slave of C. M. Pleasant. Undated. Age 13. Born Henrico Co, Va. Resides Richmond, Va. House servant.

Elizabeth. Slave of Wellington Goddin of Richmond, Va. Insured 12 January 1858.

Ellen: Born 1835, Hanover County, Va. employed Richmond, house servant. Insured by Ann Jones, 21 March 1834.

Ellicott, Andrew: Born Baltimore, Md. December 1801; Residence in Baltimore, Md. Buyer & seller of real estate. 12 April 1851.

Ellicott, Joseph: Born 1 November 1817 in Baltimore, Md. Residence in Baltimore. Flour Inspector. 11 July 1851.

Elliot, Edward G: Born Washington, D. C. 1 March 1812. Resides at Washington, D. C. U. S. Infantry 2nd. Lieutenant. 8 November 1838.

Ely, Dorsey: Born Frederick Co. Md, 24 March 1788, residence Cinncinati, Ohio, Merchant. 19 September 1831.

Emily: Birthplace not given. Age about 23. Resides in St. Louis, Missouri. A slave employed as a house servant. Insured by Charles Beardsley. 1 May 1849.

Baltimore Life Insurance Company Applications

Endicott, George: Born in Canton, Norfolk county, Massachusetts 14 June 1802. Resides in New York, N.Y. Attorney. 25 April 1836.

English, Lydia Scudder: Superintendent of a Female Seminary in Georgetown, D. C. Born and residing in Georgetown, D. C. 8 September 1852.

Ensor, George C: Born 7 May 1820, Baltimore Co. Md. Resides in Baltimore Co. Md. Farmer. Ruth Ann Ensor, spouse and beneficiary.

Ernst, D. B: Born 5 July 1815, Hanover, York County, Pennsylvania. Resides in Mercersburg, Franklin County, Pennsylvania. Student. 31 October 1840.

Estep, Alexander: Born 28 November 1785 in Maryland. Resides in Washington, D. C. Unemployed. Former Land Office employee. 18 June 1838.

Estep, Lucy M.: Born in Georgetown, District of Columbia December 1802. Resides in Calvert County, Maryland. Housewife.

Estep, T. B: Born in Charles Co., Md. February, 1822. Farmer & Planter.

Etting, Samuel: Born Baltimore, Md. 18 January 1796. Residence in Baltimore Merchant. 12 January 1844.

Evans, John: Born 14 February 1812, Portsmouth, New Hampshire. Resides in Washington, D. C. Postal clerk. 9 June 1835.

Evans/Evens, Benjamin, 56: Born Rahway, New Jersey 17 April 1800. Residence Washington, D. C. Clerk.

Faithful, William jr.: Born 8 November 1806. Bricklayer, residing in Baltimore, Maryland. 4 September 1852.

Fanny, age 17: House servant, Richmond, Virginia. Richard F. Danacott

Feddon (Feddom ?), John: Born 9 October 1826 in Fredericksburg, Va. Residence in Stafford Co. Va. Farmer. 21 July 1851.

Baltimore Life Insurance Company Applications

Feelmyer, George W.: Born in Maryland February 1831 . Resides in Ellicott Mills, Maryland. Store clerk. Intends to go to California. David Feelmyer identified as correspondent. 20 March 1849.

Fendall, Philip R: Born in Alexandria, District of Columbia 18 December 1784. Resides in Washington, D. C. Attorney. 14 May 1833.

Field, Mitchell B: Born 24 November 1808. Resides on Baltimore Street near Bond Street, Baltimore, Maryland. Court Crier and Collector.

Findley, Charles: Born in Georgetown, D. C. 24 August 1814. General Businessman, residing in Baltimore., Md.

Fine, Susannah J.: Born and resides in Fredericksburg, Virginia. Age about 30. Seamstress. Insured by John L. Knight. 5 February 1850.

Finley, Joseph Ward: Born 28 April 1801 in Baltimore, Maryland. Resides in Baltimore, Maryland. Super cargo. 8 August 1845.

Finley, Sarah A: Born in Queen Anne's County, Maryland. Age 19. Resides in Queen Anne's Co. Insured by John McKenney 12 October 1836.

Fisher, George A.: Born in Germany 9 September 1815. Resides in Washington, D. C. Baker. 12 April 1850.

Fisher, James Jr.: Born 19 June 1803, Richmond, Va. Resides in Richmond, Va. Proprietor & Superintendent of the Richmond Towing Co. Spouse, Elira D identified as beneficiary. 10 March 1836.

Fitzpatrick, John C: Born 23 November 1805 in Washington, D. C. Residence in Washington, D. C. Clerk in the office of the Secretary of the U. S. Senate. 20 March 1838.

Flanagan, Martha W: Born in Philadelphia, Pennsylvania 5 March 1835. Resides in Baltimore, Maryland. 5 May 1857.

Fleming, 13: Born Hanover Co., Va. Resides Richmond, Va. Employed at Tobacco Factory. Slave insured by William M. Sutton for Thomas Doswell.

Baltimore Life Insurance Company Applications

Fleming, William: Born 30 September 1800, Easton, Talbott County, Maryland. Resides in Baltimore, Maryland. Clerk. 22 October 1835.

Flusser, Charles T.: Born in Bohemia 1798. Resides in Annapolis, Maryland. 29 July 1833.

Foley, James S.: Born 1 October 1797 in Ireland. Residence in Petersburg, Virginia. A Tobacco manufacturer & merchant. 15 June 1844.

Foose, Edward A.: Born in Baltimore , Maryland May 1819. Resides in Baltimore, Maryland. Bricklayer. Spouse is Frances I. Going to California. 23 April 1850.

Ford, Stephen C: Born 16 October 1803, St. Mary's County, Maryland. Resides in Washington, D. C. War Department clerk. 22 February 1836.

Foreman, Moses: Born in Baltimore, Maryland 1821. Resides in District of Columbia. Will be moving to Wilmington, Delaware. House servant. Insured by Captain John Gallegher, U. S. Navy. 21 November 1835.

Forest, Mary L: Born in Baltimore, Maryland 1810. Resides in Baltimore, Maryland. Housewife. Spouse is M. L. Forest. 16 November 1835.

Forrest, Samuel: Born 21 May 1807, Georgetown, D. C. Resides in Washington, D. C. Clerk in Public Office. 24 March 1835.

Forry, Samuel Dr.: Born in Pennsylvania 23 January 1811. Resides in Frederick county, Maryland. Physician. 21 September 1836.

Foster, 15: Born Virginia. Residence in Richmond, Va. Laborer in brickyard. Insured by L. Winston, agent for Moore & Evans.

Foster, 15: Born Virginia. Resides in Richmond, Va. Laborer in brickyard. Insured by B.L. Winston, agent for Moore & Evans.

Fowler, James Martin: Born 1 June 1785, Bristol, England. Resides on St. Paul Street, Baltimore, Maryland. Accountant & Land Agent. 14 April 1841.

Baltimore Life Insurance Company Applications

Fraily, James: Born in Baltimore, Maryland 6 May 1809. Resides in Baltimore, Maryland. Midshipman, U. s. Navy. 18 June 1836.

France, Lewis H.: Born 10 March 1801, Baltimore, Maryland. Resides in Washington, D. C. Post Office Clerk. 13 March 1835.

Franciscus, John: Born December 1780. Resides in Baltimore, Maryland. 1 December 1835.

Franklin, Thomas: Born 3 April 1786, West River, Maryland (Anne Arundel County). Resides in Annapolis, Md. Cashier, Farmer's Bank of Maryland. 23 March 1837.

Freeland, Egbert: B 1787 Calvert County, Md. Resides in Baltimore, Md. Merchant. 7 February 1838.

French, Elizabeth: Born in Spotsylvania County, Virginia 14 May 1785. Resides in Fredericksburg, Virginia. Housewife.

French, Mrs. Elizabeth: Born Spotsylvania Co., Va. 26 May 1785. Widow. 30 September 1855.

French, William: Born in Amherst, New Hampshire, 1786. Resides in Washington, D. C. Post Office clerk. 15 December 1835.

Frink, Harvey: Born in Hartford, Connecticut 8 April 1800. resides in Louisville, Kentucky. Butcher. 5 May 1836.

Funk, Solomon: Born in Mansfield, Ohio in 1825. resides in Hannibal, Missouri. Cabinetmaker. 25 March 1849.

Fustug (Fustieg?), J. P.: Born 8 September 1808 in Hanover, Germany. Residence in Catonsville, Md. Storekeeper & Farmer.

Gale, Levin: 20 December 1849. Born 9 February 1824, Cecil County, Maryland. Resides in Baltimore. City, lawyer.

Gales, James: Born 10 April 1876, England. Resides in Washington, D. C. Editor. Insured by Henry C. Morgan. 20 March 1852.

Baltimore Life Insurance Company Applications

Gales, Joseph Jr.: Born in England. Age 50. Resides in Washington, D. C. Editor if the National Intelligence newspaper. 21 April 1836.

Gallagher, James: Born Wicklow, Ireland 1799. Resides at Capital Hill, Washington, D. C. Messenger.10 March 1837.

Galloway, James E.: Born in Green County, Ohio 3 January 1825. Resides in St. Louis, Missouri. Clerk. Going to California.

Gansvoort, Hun: Born in Albany, New York 17 August 1818. U. S. Navy. 20 April 1842.

Gardner, David A: Born in Morris County, New Jersey, 1794. Resides in Washington, D. C. Carpenter & undertaker. 23 April 1836.

Gardner, William H: Born in Annapolis, Maryland. Executive Officer on the ship of the line, Pennsylvania, U. S. Navy. Norfolk, Va. 7 September 1842.

Garland, Edward: Born 29 May 1809. Resides at Louisville, Kentucky. Auctioneer. 30 November 1840.

Garland, Edward: Born in Louisa County, Virginia 29 May 1809. Resides at Louisville, Kentucky. Engaged in mercantile business. 4 October 1838.

Garland, Hudson M. Jr.: Born in Virginia. Age 45. Residence in Liberty, Bedford Co., Va. John Donaldson, applicant. 1 July 1851.

Gaskins, James R: Born 26 September 1815. Resides at Baltimore, Md. Employed at Western Bank. 6 February 1837.

Gaskins, John W.: Born in Delaware 29 September 1817. resides in Baltimore, Maryland. Accountant.

Gatchel, William H.:, age 34, Born Baltimore Md. attorney. 12 March 1832.

Geganbach, John: Born 19 March 1799, Wittenberg, Germany 19 March 1799. Resides in Washington County. Farmer. Insured by William Prentiss, Washington, D. C. 27 March 1839.

Baltimore Life Insurance Company Applications

Gell, George M.: Born Baltimore, Md. 15 February 1803; residence in Baltimore, Lawyer; 20 November 1850.

George, 13: Born Chesterfield Co., Va. Slave, employed at Black Heath Coal Pits. Insured by Theodore Tompkins for William E. Martin.

George, 21: Born King William Co., Va. Residence Richmond, Va. Employed at Tobacco Factory. Slave insured by John J. Toler.

George, Robert. Born Baltimore, Md. 12 May 1822. Merchant. Residence in Baltimore. 19 October 1850.

George: Born 1815 , Hanover County, Va. Employed Va. & Tenn. R.R.

George: Born Henrico Co., Va. Age 12. Employed in tobacco factory. Lives in Richmond, Va. Insured by Thomas W. Doswell, trustee for William P. H. Davenport.

Gibbs, Thomas: Born Culpeper, Va. Age about 40. Married, waiter. Insured by Charles Herndon 7 December 1855.

Gibson, Alexander: Born 30 april 1808, Richmond, Virginia. Lieutenant in U. S. Navy, assigned to the Pacific Theater aboard the Schooner Shark. 13 July 1839.

Gibson, William D.: Born in Richmond, Virginia 26 May 1814. Resides in Richmond, Virginia. Clerk in Dry Goods Store. 7 August 1837.

Gilbert, 50: Born near Winchester, Va. Slave, employed at Black Heath Coal Pits. Insured by Theodore Tompkins for R. M. Mctyre.

Giles, Aquila P.: Born 29 July 1890 in Harford Co., Md. Residence in Baltimore, Md. Employed as a bank Clerk @ the Franklin Bank. 13 April 1844.

Giles, John (Negro): Born in St. Mary's County, Maryland. Age 26 as of December 1842. Servant /Slave owned by Seraphim Masi, Washington, D. C. Purchased by Mr. Masi to prevent separation of Giles from his family. 13 April 1842.

Baltimore Life Insurance Company Applications

Gilman, Charles Hamilton: Born in Meredith, New Hampshire 14 December 1793. . Resides in Baltimore, Maryland. Attorney.

Gilpin, Charles: Born 18 May 1812, New York, N. Y. Merchandiser and tanner, residing in Allegany County, Maryland. 1 October 1853.

Gittings, John: Born Long Green, Baltimore Co. 22 May 1798.8 March 1832.

Gittings, Lambert: Born 1 September 1806. Resides in Baltimore, Md. Merchant. 11 December 1838.

Glynn, Anthony G: Born 18 February 1787, Richmond, Va. Resides in Washington, D. C. Clerk in the Ordnance Office of the U. S. Department of War.12 January 1838.

Godey, Jane A: Born Georgetown, District of Columbia. Age 21. Resides in Georgetown, D. C. Maintains a grocery store with her spouse Walter Godey.

Goings/Goines, Richard E: Born 3 March 1818, Baltimore, Maryland. Druggisst, residing in Baltimore, Maryland. Possibly going to California. 1 April 1852.

Goode, George, 42: Born Hanover Co., Va. Employed in Grocery Store, slave. William Winston Jones, owner.

Goodwin, Arthur: Born 5 February 1802, Fredericksburg, Va. Lawyer, residing in Fredericksburg, Va. 30 January 1839.

Goodwin, Charles: Born in Fredericksburg, Virginia 30 June 1797. Resides in Baltimore, Maryland. Merchant.

Goodwin, Lyde: Born 2 November 1782 in Baltimore Arthur Pue, family physician. 12 Sept 1831

Goodwin, Lyde: Insured 21 April 1838 by letter from C. Worthington.

Gordon, Alexander George: Born in Alexandria, D. C. 1803. Resides in Virgina. U. S. Navy officer. 3 May 1836.

Baltimore Life Insurance Company Applications

Gough, Patrick (Negro): Born St. Mary's County, Maryland. Resides in Baltimore when not at sea. Seaman, insured by Mary Sloan. 23 December 1835.

Gould, James F.: Born 24 November 1791 in Boston, Massachusetts. Resides in Baltimore, Maryland. Teacher. Jane Gould, spouse. 31 December 1849.

Gould, James: Born 1795, Massachusetts. Jewelry salesman, residing in Baltimore, Maryland. 28 April 1853.

Gould, James: Born at Beverly, Massachusetts 28 August 1793. Resides in Baltimore, Md. Seaman on the brig ' Niobe', sailing from Baltimore to Africa 1 November 1836. 24 February 1837.

Gould, James: Born in Beverly, Massachusetts 28 August 1793. Resides in Baltimore, Maryland. Trader. Returning from African coast. 24 December 1835.

Gould, James: Born in Beverly, Massachusetts 30 March 1795. Resides in Baltimore, Md. Storekeeper. 4 August 1832.

Gould, John: Born 15 June 1795, London, England. Resides in Washington, D. C. Clerk in the Attorney General's office. 29 December 1836.

Graff, Frederick C: Born 2 March 1780 in Germany. Resides in Baltimore, Maryland. Merchant. 14 May 1833.

Graham, Thomas J.: Born 11 January 1818 in Baltimore, Maryland. Resides in Baltimore, Maryland. Druggist. 8 Januarys 1849.

Gray, Jane Mrs.: Housewife, Born in Virginia, residing in Stafford County, Virginia at 'Traveler's Rest". Spouse is John Gray. 20 September 1852.

Green, Joshua Jr.: Born in Harford County, Maryland 18 July 1811. Resides in Havre de Grace, Maryland. Planning to move to Mississippi, Missouri, or Kansas. Druggist. 16 September 1835.

Griffith, Romulus R: Born 9 June 1803, Montgomery Co., Md. Hardware merchant, residing in Baltimore Co., Md. 24 March 1852.

Baltimore Life Insurance Company Applications

Grigsby, Francis Frost: Born 25 January 1816 in Clarke Co., Va. Resides in Clarke Co., Va. Farmer's Wife. Spouse is Henry N. Grigsby. 23 March 1850.

Grover, Charles: Born Baltimore County, Maryland June 1794. Resides in Baltimore, Maryland. Lumber merchant. 19 September 1832.

Grubb, Sam: Born in Shepherdstown, Jefferson County, Virginia 10 November 1796. Resides in Washington, D. C. Messenger in the office of the Auditor of the U. S. Treasury. 31 August 1836.

Guilteau Rev. L.: 23 March 1834.

Gwathney, Samuel: Born King William Co. Virginia 22 January 1779. residence Louisville, Ky. 12 June 1839.

Gwynn, John R.: Born 14 February 1812. Residence in Baltimore, Md. Mercantile Trader. 1 September 1851.

Gwynn, William: Born in Tyrone County, Ireland 12 December 1775. Resides in Baltimore, Maryland. Attorney, Newspaper Editor. 19 April 1834. .

Hagner, Alexander B: Born 13 July 1826 in Washington D. C. Resides in Annapolis, Md. Lawyer.

Hagner, John R.: Born 26 March 1811 in Washington, D. C. Resides in Washington, D. C. U. S. Army Paymaster. 21 March 1850

Hagner,Alexander: Born 13 July 1826 in Washington D. C. Residence in Annapolis, Md. Lawyer.

Haines, Charles: 39: Born Windsor, England 22 August 1825. Residence 127 Ann St, Baltimore, Md. Seaman.

Haines, Charles: 39: Born Windsor, England 22 August 1825. Resides 127 Ann St, Baltimore, Md. Seaman.

Hale Phillip: Born March 1804, Baltimore, Maryland. Residence is Baltimore, Md. Sea Captain. 2 October 1834.

Baltimore Life Insurance Company Applications

Hale, William H: Born 15 March 1811, Baltimore, Maryland. Resides in Baltimore @8650 Howard Street. Bricklayer. 15 June 1852. (Possibly going to California).

Hall, Caroline: Born in King George County, Virginia. Age about 35/36. Resides in Washington, District of Columbia. A former slave who had sold, but was repurchased by a friend, one Dr. Phineas T. Bradley, who is insuring her to secure the purchase money advanced. 7 May 1839.

Hall, Francis C: Born Queen Anne's County, Maryland 14 November 1784. Resides in Philadelphia, Pennsylvania. Marine Corp. officer. 13 February 1836.

Hall, Joseph: B 1819, Culpepper City, Virginia. Resides in Fredericksburg, Va. Carpenter. 22 January 1852.

Hall, Richard W.: Born in England 4 August 1781. Resides in Baltimore, Maryland. Clerk. 10 September 1832.

Hall, W. Kent: Born 22 February 1828, Baltimore, Maryland. Merchant, residing in Baltimore, Maryland. Insurance is made payable to P. Henry Sullivan. 6 March 1853.

Hammond, Charles: Born in Boston, Massachusetts 27 February 1810. Resides in Baltimore, Maryland. Apothecary. 19 November 1834.

Hammond, Richard P: Born October 1820, Washington County, Maryland. Customs Collector, residing in San Francisco, California. 16 April 1859.

Hampton, Robert B: Born in Virginia, Resides in California, Age abot 36. Insured by R. H. Love of Baltimore, Maryland. 13 May 1852.

Hands, Washington: Born 12 March 1808, Baltimore, Maryland. Resides Baltimore, Maryland. Sea Captain. 18 October 1848.

Handy, John H. Born 30 November 1830 in Somerset Co., Md. Residence in Baltimore, Md.

Baltimore Life Insurance Company Applications

Handy, John Jr.: Born Ann Arundel county, Md. February 1813. Resides in Washington, D. C. Unemployed. Insured by Edmund James 13 April 1838.

Handy, Levin: Born 20 December 1813, Snow Hill, Maryland. Resides at Washington, D. C. Officer, U. S. Navy. 20 December 1838.

Handy, William: Born 18 January 1816, Snow Hill, Maryland. Resides in Washington, D. C. Clerk in the office of the U. S. Comptroller. 5 June 1839.

Hanna, William: Born Baltimore, Md., 22 October 1806. Residence in Baltimore, Md., Clerk at Savings Bank of Baltimore. Beneficiary is Ann Purnell Hanna, wife. 14 February 1851.

Hanson, Isaac K: Born Alexandria, District of Columbia 14 January 1790. Resides in Washington, D. C. Clerk in Registrar's Office of the Department of the Treasury. 7 May 1834.

Hardesty, C. R: Born Calvert Co. 6 April 1797. d. 9 July 1862. 6 February 1838.

Hardie, Robert: Born 17 June 1798 in Philadelphia, Pa. Residence in Baltimore, Maryland. Grocer.

Hardy, Robert: Born Bedford Co., Va. Age 8. Slave, employed as a house servant. Resides in Richmond, Va. Insured by C.Ballauss.

Hardy, Thomas Dr: Born 1828, Petersburg, Ohio. Resides Baltimore, Maryland. Physician.

Harman, John: Born 23 September 1798. Resides in Baltimore, Maryland. Tobacconist. January 1838. Benefits payable to Ellen P., Mary Louisa, and Margaret P. Harman.

Harper, Francis: Born 1 October 18129, Ireland. Resides in the District of Columbia. Banking House Clerk. 20 May 1856.

Harriet: Born in Baltimore, Maryland July 1822. Resides in Baltimore, Md. Slave employed as a house servant. Insured by Nicholas Brewer 2 June 1834.

Baltimore Life Insurance Company Applications

Harris, Carey A.: Born Wilson County, Tennessee, 23 September 1806. Resides in Georgetown, D. C. Chief Clerk of U. S. Department of War. 2 July 1834, 12 June 1835.

Harris, Edgar 13: Born Powhatan, Va. Resides in Powhatan. Slave, employed as factory worker. Insured by John Darracott.

Harris, Edgar: Born Powhatten County, age 42, shoemaker, Richmond, Virginia.

Harrison, Alexander Born: 12 December 1848, Baltimore, Maryland. Resides in Franklin County, Indiana. Machinist. 29 October 1849.

Harrison, Gustavius: Age 22. Resides in Washington, D. C. employed at U. S. Naval Observatory. 12 December 1848.

Harrison, Gustavus: Born 11 January 1791, Prince William County, Virginia. Resides at Georgetown, District of Columbia. Clerk . 6 July 1839.

Harrison, Horace N: Born in Georgia, 1808. Officer in U. S. Navy. 1 August 1835.

Harrison, Samuel S: Born in Fredericksburg, Va. 2 September 1826. Bank Officer, residing in Fredericksburg, Va. 25 May 1857.

Harrison, Thomas P: Born 7 February 1802, Kent Island, Queen Anne's county, Md. Resides in Baltimore, Maryland. General Clerk for Philip Littig, attorney. 29 December 1837.

Harrison, William H.: Born 15 May 1810, Amelia County, Virginia. Resides in Amelia County. Schoolmaster. 10 July 1835. Letter requesting an increase in coverage from $1000 to $5000, effective 1 February 1837. Richmond, Va. 9 January 1837.

Harrison: Slave insured by L. Hilliary: in possession of Jacob Fechtig, to indemnify Joseph Everstine against personal losses in administration of the estate of Margaret Hilliary. 25 October 1834. Cumberland, Maryland.

Baltimore Life Insurance Company Applications

Harry: Born 1799, Fauquier County, Virginia. To remove to Cooper County, Missouri. Blacksmith. A slave originally owned by one Thomas Fisher, sold to and insured by Henry L. Pope ($1000). 27 September 1837.

Hart, W: Born in Connecticut 1797. Insured by Pairo & Mourse, attorneys of Washington, D. C.

Hart, W: Born. 1797 in Conn. Insured by Pairo & Mourse, attorneys, Washington D. C.

Hawkins, H. L: Letter from Fort Severn, Annapolis, Md. Renewing policy. 4 February 1836.

Haywood, Thomas: Born 15 October 1796, eastern shore of Maryland. Resides Tallahassee, Florida. Merchant & Farmer. 7 April 1849.

Heald, John R.: Born 31 May 1829, Baltimore, Maryland. Resides Baltimore, Maryland. Tobacco & cigar merchant. 20 October 1850.

Heiner, Elias: Born Carroll Co, Md. Resides in Baltimore, Md., minister. 5 October 1855.

Heiner, John: Born 27 May 1815, Uniontown, Carroll County, Maryland. Resides at Moorsville, Indiana. Physician. Insured by Elias Heiner 30 August 1841.

Henry, 14: Born Chesterfield Co., Va. Slave, employed at Black Heath Coal Pits. Insured by Theodore Tompkins for R. M. Mctyre..

Henry, 40: Born Chesterfield Co., Va. Slave, employed at Black Heath Coal Pits. Insured by James L. Porter.

Henry, a slave: Age 22, employed in Tobacco Factory in Richmond, Va. Insured by Benjamin Temple.

Henry, William age 10: Born Hanover, Va. works in brickyard in Richmond, Va. April 1834. J. P. Talley, Richmond, Va.

Henry. Slave of L. Winston of Richmond, Va. Insured 18 April 1857.

Henry: Born 1835 in Va. laborer on Va. & Tenn. RR.

Baltimore Life Insurance Company Applications

Henry: 18 April 1857. Slave of L. Winston of Richmond, Va. $500.

Hepburn, John W: Born 3 January 1790, near Annapolis, Maryland. General Government clerk. 16 May 1835.

Herbert: Slave of George Whitlock. Tobacconist, married, resides in Richmond, Va.

Herndon, Brodie S: Physician, Born (7 July 1810) and residing in Fredericksburg, Virginia. 13 March 1841, 29 March 1853.

Herring, Henry: Born Baltimore, Maryland. Age 59. Resides in Baltimore, Md. Operates a steam boat planning mill. 30 January 1852.

Hickman, N.: Born 1797 in Delaware. Resides in Baltimore, Md. Register of Wills for Baltimore City. 5 December 1851.

Higgins, Edward: Born October 1821, Norfolk, Virginia. Resides in Baltimore, Maryland. Naval officer. 4 June 1849.

Hilberg, Frederick: Born 31 August 1815, Germany. Resides in Baltimore, Maryland. Tailor. Insured by Francis L. Hilberg, spouse 15 April 1839.

Hilton, William Born: Born 22 April 1826, Wiscaful, Maine. Resides in Jersey City, New Jersey. Ships master. Harriet Born Hilton, mother. 1 December 1849.

Hindman, William: Born on Eastern Shore of Maryland November 1792. Resides in Baltimore, Maryland. Merchant. 10 August 1832.

Hines, Isaac: Born 20 April 1795, Kent county, Maryland. Resides in Baltimore, Maryland. Book Keeper at the Merchants Bank of Baltimore. 30 December 1836.

Hitch, Sarah (Mrs.): Born Baltimore, Md. Oct. 1898. Residence in Baltimore Application completed by William G. Krebs, trustee February 1851.

Hitchcock, Ira Irving: Born February 1793 in Hirkimas Co., N.Y. 14 May 1833.

Baltimore Life Insurance Company Applications

Hobson, George B: Born in New York, N. Y 22 January 1803. Resides at Valparaiso, Chile. 11 August 1838.

Hodgkin, Theodore: Born 16 April 1808, Calvert co., Md. Resides Calvert Co., Md. Farmer. 2 April 1849.

Hogg, John W: Born 13 May 1828, Nashville, Tennessee. Clerk at the U. S. Department of Treasury, residing in Washington, D. C. 18 July 1853.

Hogg. John W: Born Nashville, Tenn. 13 May 1828. Resides in Washington, D. C. Office Clerk. 11 July 1855.

Holland, John C.: Born 24 January 1822, Baltimore, Maryland. Resides in Baltimore, Md. at # 48 N. Gay Street. Paperhanger & upholsterer. 18 February 1846.

Hollander, John: Born in Germany 11 August 1803. Resides in Louisville, Kentucky. Dry Goods Merchant. 31 August 1838.

Holmead, Anthony: Born 25 December 1799, Washington, D. C. Resides in Washington, D. C. Dry goods merchant. 30 April 1838.

Holmes, Mead: Born 1 May 1796, Rutland, Vermont. Resides Granville Township, Licking Co., Ohio. Farmer.

Holter, Lewis: Born St. Jago, Cuba10 December. 1803. Resides in Balto., Md. Cooper. 13 July 1837. Reinsured 26 October 1850.

Homans, Benjamin: Born in Bordeaux, France September 1799. Resides in Georgetown, D. C. Newspaper editor and Fire Insurance company secretary. 21 June 1832.

Hoomes, Robert: Born in or near Fredericksburg, Va. Age about 30. Residence in Richmond, Va. A slave employed as brick maker. Insured by his owner John L. Marye (Mayo/ Mary) 4 July 1849.

Hooper, Robert: Born 25 December 1812, Baltimore, Maryland. An accountant, residing in Baltimore, Maryland. 21 June 1841.

Baltimore Life Insurance Company Applications

Hoover, Francis J.: Born 28 September 1810, Emmetsburg, Md. Resides in Emmetsburg, Md. Has wife & 5 children. Silversmith. 28 February 1849.

Hopkins, James: Born 9 November 1807. Resides in Baltimore, Maryland. 15 June 1837.

Horace, 25: Born Chesterfield Co., Va. Slave, employed at Black Heath Coal Pits. Insured by Theodore Tompkins for William E. Martin.

Horstman, John C: B 3 January 1796, Baltimore, Maryland. House carpenter residing in Baltimore, Md. Possibly going to California.

Howard, Charles Jr.: Born 6 February 1830, Baltimore, Maryland. Resides in Alexandria, Virginia. Married. Merchant. 11 October 1856.

Howard, Flodoardo: Born 11 March 1811, Stafford County, Virginia. Resides, Washington, D. C. Druggist. 21 June 1833.

Howard, John E: Born 1821. Applicant is Augustus Warner. 25 July 1831.

Howard. Marion: Born Richmond, Va. 1825. Resides in Richmond, Va. Physician. 14 July 1855.

Hudgin, Robert: Born 10 August 1802, Fredericksburg, Virginia. Resides in Bowling Green, Virginia. Clerk of the Caroline county, Virginia Circuit Court.

Hume, Ebenezer James: Born near Nashville, Tennessee 29 December 1806. Resides in Washington, D. C. Clerk in the U.S. Treasury Department.

Hunter, Charles G.: Born Trenton, New Jersey, 9 November 1807. Resides in Bordertown, New Jersey. U. S. Navy. Lieutenant. 23 February 1838.

Hunter, Taliaferro; Born 25 January 1811 in Virginia. Residence in Frederick (Fredericksburg ??), Va. Public Works Contractor. 20 May 1851.

Hussey, Asahel: Born July 1782 in New York . Resides in Baltimore, Md. Innkeeper. 21 September 1835.

Baltimore Life Insurance Company Applications

Ingleson, John C: B 19 June 1826, Baltimore, Maryland. , Baltimore, Maryland. House Peddler residing in Baltimore, Md. Possibly going to California. 5 February 1852

Irving, Levin J: Born 27 August 1807, Somerset County, Maryland. Resides in Worcester, County, Maryland. Farmer. 7 May 1841.

Irwin, James S.: Born Farminough, Ireland, December 1805; residence Louisville, Ky. 12 June 1839

Israel, 34: Slave employed in Tobacco factory. Resides in Richmond, Va. Insured by J. H. T. Mayo. 5 February 1857.

Jack: Born 1 May 1811, Williamsport, Maryland. Resides in Williamsport, Maryland. Slave employed as a House servant. Insured by W. L. Compton. 15 July 1835.

Jackson, Andrew M. D: Born 3 March 1801, Orange County, New York. Resides at Norfolk, Virginia. Purser, U. S. Navy. 31 January 1837.

Jackson, Andrew R.: Born 16 May 1815 in Muskegon Co., Ohio. Residence in Louisville, Ohio. Surveyor. 9 August 1851.

Jackson, Andrew: Slave, employed as a hostler and servant by Robert Morfit. Insured by John Inglehart 31 August 1852.

Jackson, John A.: Born 2 January 1814, Baltimore, Maryland. Resides on Eden street in Baltimore, Maryland. Silversmith.

Jackson, Robert: Born Calvert Co., Md. about 1817. Resides in Baltimore, Md. A sailor.

Jackson, Washington: Born in Ireland, January 1784. Resides in Philadelphia, Pennsylvania. Merchant. 2 May 1837.

Jacobs, Newman M: B June 1806, Front royal, Va. Merchant residing in Front Royal. Va. 25 April 1853.

Jacobs, Robert T: Born 17 January 1803, Queen Ann's County, Maryland. Postal clerk. 19 June 1839.

Jakes, Ralph, colored man: Insured by Henry Jakes of Baltimore, Maryland. No other data given.

Baltimore Life Insurance Company Applications

Jakes, Ralph: Born October, 1822 in Baltimore, Md. En route to California. Insured by Henry Jakes 21 September 1851.

James, 12: Born King William Co., Va. Residence Richmond, Va. Employed at Tobacco Factory. Slave insured by John J. Toler.

James, a slave: age 35. Residence in Kanawasha, Va. Employed in mines. Insured by C. S. G. Noland.

James, a slave: Born in Caroline Co. Age about 44. Employed in a Tobacco factory.

James, a slave: Born in Caroline Co. Age about 44. Employed in a Tobacco factory.

James, John Dawson: Born in Washington, D. C. 1805. Resides in Washington, D. C. Clerk. 13 June 1849.

James, William: Born 9 June 1800, Philadelphia, Pennsylvania. Resides in Washington, D. C. Clerk at the Office of Registry, U. S. Treasury. 9 December 1835.

James: Born King William County, Virginia May 1833. Slave, residing in Henrico County, Virginia, insured by Robert H. Broaddus 28 May 1852.

James: Born, Calvert County, Maryland. Resides in Calvert County, Maryland. A slave insured by Benjamin Worrell/Morrell. 20 September 1850.

Jamison, Ann: Born Dorchester Co., Md. 15 December 1814. Residence in Baltimore, Md. Merchant. 1 October 1849.

Jane: 29 October 1853. Born about 1833 in Queen Anne's County, Maryland.

Janney, William H.: Born Alexandria, DC. 23 October 1824. Residence in Baltimore, Md. Merchant. 11 September 1851.

Janvier, Thomas: Born 1 July 1791, Cape Francois, St. Domingo Resides in Baltimore, Md. Super Cargo. 18 January 1834.

Jarrett, Abraham Lingan: Born in Harford Co., Md. In September or October, 1808. Residence in Bel Air, Harford Co., Md. Employed as deputy clerk. 17 July 1851.

Baltimore Life Insurance Company Applications

Jay, John O: Born Stafford County, Virginia 20 February 1815. Resides at Falmouth, Virginia. Attorney at Law. 24 July 1839.

Jefferson, 22: Born Chesterfield, Va. Slave, employed at Black Heath Coal Pits. Insured by Theodore Tompkins for William E. Martin.

Jencks, Theodore Russell: Born 24 December 1802, Cambridge, Massachusetts. Resides in Baltimore, Maryland, Teacher. 31 January 1835.

Jenkins, George Taylor: Born Orange Co., Va. Born 1813. Resides in Baltimore, Md. In mercantile business. 29 September 1855.

Jenkins, Elizabeth: Born 16 October 1820 in Baltimore, Maryland. Resides in Baltimore, Md. Insured by G. Taylor Jenkins 18 October 1850.

Jerry: Born in Alabama in 1821 or 1822. Resides in Washington, D. C. A slave employed as a house servant. Insured by Arthur P. Bagby 4 September 1849.

Jerry: Born May 1827, Caroline County, Virginia. Slave, employed as a house servant, insured by Robert H. Broaddus 26 May 1852.

Jewett, Joseph: Born at Baltimore, Maryland 10 November 1810. Resides in Baltimore. U. S. Navy Lieutenant. 10 March 1842.

Jim, 29: Born Spotsylvania Co, Va. Resides in Richmond, Va. Dining Room Servant. D. Lee Powell, insurer.

Jim, a slave: Born Hanover County., Va. , age about 20. Employed on Danville R.R.

Joe, 14: Born Hanover, Va. Resides in Richmond, Va. Slave employed in brickmaking. Insured by William O. Winston for the benefit of Mrs. E. Christian & children, owners.

Joe, 15: Born King & Queen Co. Va. Residence in Richmond, Va. Slave, employed in brickyard. Insured by L. Winston, agent for F. Govern.

Joe: Born about 1825, Charles City, Chesterfield, Va. Slave of William A. Marston employed as a woodcutter and teamster.

Baltimore Life Insurance Company Applications

Joe: Born in Williamsport, Maryland 1 May 1811. Slave employed as a house servant. Insured by William L. Compton, Williamsport, Md. 15 July 1835.

John H. Handy: Born. 30 November 1830 in Somerset co., Md. Resides in Baltimore City. 12 November 1853.

John, age 13: Born Richmond, resides Richmond, employed in tobacco factory. Thomas Pollard, applicant. 6 April 1834.

John: A slave insured by Samuel Gittings for 4 years. 30 November 1837.

John: Age 25. Born in Calvert County, Maryland. A slave insured by Edward Reynolds 13 August 1850.

John: Born Henrico County, 1842, laborer Va. & Tenn RR. , 31 March 1834. L. Winston, applicant

John: Born Henrico County, Va. Resides in Prince Edward County, Va. Slave working on railroad construction. (Southside Railroad. Insured by Samuel Cottrell. 16 February 1852.

Johnson, Dennis, 30: Born Westmoreland Co, Va. Residence Westmoreland Co., Va. Being shipped to Louisiana. Slave Insured by William D. Nelson.

Johnson, Dennis, 30: Born Westmoreland Co, Va. Resides Westmoreland Co., Va. Being shipped to Louisiana. Slave Insured by William D. Nelson.

Johnson, Eliphalet: Born in Fitzwilliam, New Hampshire 28 August 1803. Resides in Baltimore, Maryland. 16 July 1835.

Johnson, Eliza: ("colored girl"): Born Baltimore, Md. Age about 3.5 years. Residence & will be employed in the home of John Cooper, applicant. (Most likely a slave.) 15 April 1851.

Johnson, James, colored. Insured by George W. Worthington of Howard Co., Md. 13 April 1853.

Johnson, James: Farmhand, Born and residing in Howard County, Maryland. 6 August 1852.

Johnson, Reverdy: Born 21 May 1796, Annapolis, Md. Lawyer, residing in Baltimore, Md. Insured 3 March 1832, 22 March 1833, 27 June 1853.

Baltimore Life Insurance Company Applications

Johnston, Fayette: Born in Stafford County, Virginia. Age about 38. resides in Fredericksburg, Va. Dry Goods merchant. 25 June 1833.

Johnston, Francis: Born in England 23 December 1813. Ladies shoemaker, residing at #43 Lexington St., Baltimore, Md.

Johnston, Gabriel: Born 21 May 1808, Fredericksburg, Virginia. Resides in Fredericksburg, Virginia. Auctioneer. 26 May 1849.

Johnston, John, 18 Born Caroline Co., Va. Residence Fredericksburg, Va. Slave. Insured by William White.

Johnston, Robert N.: Born Baltimore 29 October 1788. Assistant to the Clerk of House of Representatives of U.S. Wife Maria V. 27 Sept. 1831.

Johnston, Virginia Elizabeth: Born Boston, Mass 19 December 1829. Insured by George W. Dobbin, trustee. 17 October 1855.

Jonathan Meredith: Born 4 October 1784. Residence Baltimore, Md. practicing attorney. 3 September 1832.

Jones, Brims: Born 18 October 1810, Brunswick County, Virginia. Resides at Petersburg, Virginia. Commission House clerk. 24 August 1832.

Jones, George W: Born Charleston, Jefferson Co, Va. 1827. Residence in Richmond, dentist.

Jones, Walter F: Born in Hanover County, Virginia. Resides in Norfolk, Virginia. Master of Port of Norfolk. 5 October 1835.

Jones, Warner: Born 10 January 1798, Lynchburg, Virginia. Resides in New Glasgow, Amherst, Virginia. Physician. 18 January 1838.

Jordan, William M: Born Baltimore, Maryland 5 November 1814. Resides in Harford County, Maryland. Farmer. 24 February 1849.

Joshua, a slave: Born Chesterfield Co. , Va. Employed in Richmond, Va. As a tobacco box maker. Insured by J. P. Winston. No date.

Baltimore Life Insurance Company Applications

Joyce, Henry & John: 2 April 1857, Henry Born Ireland 6 April 1818. Grocer in Washington D. C. No information on John I. Joyce.

Jubah: Born Henrico County, Va. Resides in Prince Edward County, Va. Slave working on railroad construction (Southside Railroad. Insured by Samuel Cottrell. 16 February 1852.

Julius F. Heileman:, U. S. Army Officer, stationed @ Sullivan's Island, S. C. Born Granville, Hamden Co. Mass.5 October 1831.

Kahissowski, Henry K.: Born 11 September 1807, Poland. Resides in Washington, D. C. Clerk. 17 October 1855.

Kane, Rufus K.: Born 28 May 1819, Maryland. Resides in Baltimore, Maryland. Bricklayer. Going to California. 29 March 1850.

Katz, Marcus: Born 1825, Germany. Resides in Baltimore, Maryland. Dry Goods Dealer. Going to California. 1 April 1850.

Keeling, David F.: Born in Princess Anne County, Virginia. Resides in Norfolk, Va. Innkeeper. 4 September 1850.

Keller, Charles M.: Born in France 12 June 1810. Resides in Georgetown, District of Columbia. Patent Office clerk. 2 September 1836.

Kellogg, John H: Born in Keene, New Hampshire 7 February 1804. Resides in Louisville, ___. General agent for the 'Comprehensive Commentary'. 29 March 1836.

Kellum, Edward M: Born on the Eastern Shore of Maryland. Age about 35. Resides in Baltimore, Maryland. Carpenter. Going to California.

Kennard, Alexander A: Born 30 May 1806, Kent County, Maryland. Resides in Baltimore, Maryland. Justice of the Peace of Baltimore City.10 March 1838.

Kerr, John Bozman: Born 5 March 1809 in Easton, Md. Residence in Easton, Md. Employed as Congressional Representative for the 6th District of Maryland.

Baltimore Life Insurance Company Applications

Keyworth, Robert, Born March 1795, South Leverton, Nottingham, England. Silversmith, residence in Washington, D.C.

King, J. D.: Born Georgetown April 1797. Residence in Washington, D. C. Employed as clerk at the U. S. State Dept. 11 February 1851.

King, James D: Born 24 April 1797, Georgetown, District of Columbia. Resides at Georgetown, District of Columbia. Clerk in the "5th. Central Auditor's Office. 6 March 1839.

Kitzmiller, Archibald M: Born in Leesburg, Loudon county, Virginia. Resides in Leesburg, Virginia. Will be removing to Harper's Ferry, Jefferson City, Virginia. Lawyer. 26 May 1836.

Klockeither, Lewis: Born 13 February 1817, Baltimore, Maryland. Resides in Baltimore, Maryland at Howard and Mulberry Streets. Clerk. 30 January 1849.

Kortwright, Cornelius H.: Born 20 September 1811, St. Croix, Born W. I. Resides in Puerto Rico. Estate Proprietor. 19 November 1849.

Krager, Henry: Born 11 February 1819, Baltimore, Maryland. Resides in Baltimore, Maryland. Bricklayer. 12 January 1849.

Krebs, Charles W.: Born 21 August 1803, Baltimore, Maryland. Resides in Baltimore, Md. Also has a second residence in New York. Merchant. 9 October 1848.

Krudenis, Paul Baron: Born 31 January 1784. Resides in Washington, D. C. 20 January 1834.

Kurtz, J. D: U. S. Army officer Born and residing in Georgetown, District of Columbia. Birthdate is 27 April 1820.

Lackland, M. C.: Born in Buckingham County, Virginia 20 February 1795. Resides in Richmond, Virginia. Tobacco Inspector. 25 April 1835.

Lafitte, Henry Born: Born 5 January 1822, Baltimore, Maryland. Resides in Baltimore, Md. Merchant. Plans to go to California. 3 March 1850.

Baltimore Life Insurance Company Applications

Landis, Joseph A: Born 26 June 1806, Pennsylvania. Resides in Alexandria, La. Physician. 14 November 1836.

Larned, Charles H: Born in Providence, Rhode Island. Age 30. U. S. Army Officer. Application completed in Washington, D. C. 21 January 1841.

Latrobe, John H: Born 4 May 1803. Resides in Baltimore, Maryland. Traveling to Natchez, Mississippi, & New Orleans, La. 20 October 1834.

Lattimans, Alexander Frederick: Resides in Brazil. Insured by Robert Clinton Wright 29 June 1842. No personal data given on applicant or insured. Application is by letter.

Laurence, Col. A. N: Born in New York 6 December 1793.Importer of Wines, residing in Baltimore, Md. 21 August 1857.

Laurensen, James: Born 22 March 1803, Bristol, England. Resides in Washington, D. C. Postal clerk. 27 November 1851.

Laurie, Cranston: Born 14 July 1809, Washington, D. C. Resides in Washington, D. C. Postal clerk. 8 February 1836.

Lavinia, 14: Born Goochland Co., Va. Residence in Richmond, Va. Slave employed as a house servant. Insured by Archibald Bolling. 5 February 1857.

Law, James Owen: Born 14 March 1809, Baltimore, Maryland. Resides in Baltimore. Miller. 19 July 1842.

Lawson, Nancy Jane: Born in Richmond, Va. Age 14.Slave insured by John B. Crenshaw, employed as a nurse in the household. Resides in Henrico Co. Va. On owners farm. Reinsured at age 15.

Lawson, Fanny: Born in Richmond, Va. Age 10. Slave, employed by John B. Crenshaw as a house servant in Richmond, Va. Reinsured at age 16.

Lawson, Henry, Jr: Born, Baltimore., Md. Age 12. Slave, drives milk cart for John B. Crenshaw. Reinsured by Crenshaw at age 16.

Baltimore Life Insurance Company Applications

Lawson, Kitty, 8: Born Richmond, Va., in 1829. Residence in Henrico Co., Va. Employed as House girl. Insured by John Born Crenshaw. 14 February 1857.

Lawson, Mary Ann: Born in Richmond, Va. Age 16. Slave, insured by John B. Crenshaw, employed as a washerwoman, residing in Richmond, Va. Reinsured at age 15.

Lea, Albert Miller: Born 23 July 1808. Resides in Baltimore, Maryland. Engineer on the Baltimore & Ohio Railroad. 9 May 1839.

Leary, Cornelius. L. L.: Born Baltimore, Md. 22 October 1813. Resides Ann St, Baltimore, Md., Lawyer. 19 July 1849.

Leary, Thomas H. H.: Born 3 January 1816, Baltimore, Maryland. Resides in Baltimore, Maryland. Book Keeper. Application undated.

Leary, William B: Born County Cork, Ireland, June 1796. Resides in Annapolis, Md. Removing to Greenville, S. C. Teacher. 14 March 1837.

Lee, Catherine: Born in Maryland. Age 40. Spouse of Major Lee of Illinois. Insured by Ignatius Baurman 6 January 1838.

Lehmanousky, Edward: Born 13 May 1795, Warshaw (Warsaw), Poland. Resides in Washington, D. C. Postal clerk. 2 March 1836.

Lendrum, Thomas W., Born 24 November 1792. Officer, U. S. Army (major). 21 ___ 1838

Leonard, William T. Dr.: Born 22 October1810, Cambridge, Maryland. Resides in Baltimore, Maryland. U. S. Army physician being assigned to Fort French, Louisiana. 11 September 1838.

Levin, L. C.: No data given. Insurance renewed by letter from C. W. Pairo, Washington, D. C. 28 March 1848.

Levin, Lewis C: Congressional Representative, Born in South Carolina 1810. Resides in Philadelphia, Pennsylvania. 18 December 1852.

Baltimore Life Insurance Company Applications

Lewis, Edward W: Born 25 October 1801, District of Columbia. Resides in the District of Columbia. Clerk in the 2nd. Auditor's Office, U. S. Treasury Department. 3 June 1839.

Lewis, John T.: Born 22 January 1816, Culpepper County, Virginia. Resides in Caroline County, Virginia. Farmer. 22 March 1849.

Lewis, William: Born in Prince William County, Virginia. Age about 24. Resides in Alexandria, D. C. A slave employed as a laborer, cart man, or baker. Insured by William H. Miller 13 June 1836.

Lightner, James: Born 9 June 1820, Augusta County, Virginia. Resides in Lexington, Missouri. 7 March 1849.

Ligin, James: Born February 1789, Powhaten Co., Va. Resides at Petersburg, Va. Clerk at the Petersburg Railroad, Co. 21 January 1839.

Lindsey, G. F.: Born Prince William County, Virginia. Resides in Philadelphia, Pennsylvania. Lieutenant, U. S. Marines. 21 September 1835.

Linville, Maria: Born 17 March 1799 in Baltimore, Maryland. Resides on Gay Street, Baltimore, Maryland. Insured by Frederick Fitch 26 July 1831.

Litle, Charles: Born in Philadelphia, Pennsylvania 16 February 1797. Resides in Washington, D. C. Employed by the Federal Government. 1 August 1836.

Little, Andrew M: Born 20 January 1826, Warren County, New Jersey. Engaged in the Timber business in King George County, Virginia. 1 October 1852.

Little, David M: Born 23 June 1813, Philadelphia, Pennsylvania. Resides in Richmond, Virginia. Book Keeper. 26 April 1839.

Livingston, James: Born November 1816, Porta Ferry, Ireland. Resides in Versailles, Missouri. Engaged in mining. 3 March 1849.

Lomax, P. Thornton: Born Fredericksburg, Va. 2 March 1820, lawyer, resides in Fredericksburg, Virginia. 30 August 1848

Baltimore Life Insurance Company Applications

London: Born Hanover County, age 24, resides in Dinwiddie, employed in coalfields.

Long, Cornelius Born: Born 13 February 1813, Baltimore, Maryland. Resides in Baltimore, Md. Spouse is Frances A. Long. Ship Master En route to Rotterdam. 3 October 1849.

Long, Ellis B: Born in Frederick County, Virginia 21 June 1807. Resides in Baltimore, Maryland. Dry Goods merchant. 21 November 1842.

Loughery, A. S.: Born Versailles, Kentucky January 1810. Resides in Washington, D. C. Clerk. 8 October 1849.

Louisa, 22: House servant, Richmond, Virginia. Richard F. Danacott.

Lowery, James H.: Born July 1794, Georgetown, District of Columbia. Resides in Washington, D. C. Clerk. 29 September 1849.

Lownes, J. H. D.: Born 14 May 1809 Richmond, Va. Resides in Richmond, Va. Occupation is illegible. 13 February 1838.

Loyall, William: Born 18 January 1794, Norfolk, Virginia. Resides in Norfolk, Virginia. Revenue Inspector. 28 May 1838.

Lucas, Charles: B Fredericksburg, Va. Age about 25. Resides on the Rappahannock River. Slave.

Lucas, Ellen: Born April 1824, Maryland. Resides in Washington, D. C. Blacksmith.

Lucas, James: Born 10 May 1795, Baltimore, Maryland. Resides in Baltimore, Maryland. Printer. 23 April 1842.

Luce, John B: Born 2 February 1816, Albany, New York. Resides at Washington, D. C. Clerk in the Office of Indian Affairs. 2 February 1839.

Lucy, age 12: Born Henrico County, Va. J. P. Talley, Richmond, Va.

Ludwig, Samuel: B 13 February 1801, Hungary. Publisher, residing in Baltimore, Maryland. @107 E. Baltimore Street. 1 March 1852.

Baltimore Life Insurance Company Applications

Lussborough, Harriet: Born 25 May 1809 in Montgomery County, Maryland. Resides in Montgomery County, Maryland. 3 November 1852.

Lyles, Barbara Ann: Widow. Born and residing in Anne Arundel County, Maryland. Birthdate is given as 1890.

Lyman, William O: Born Boston, Massachusetts, June 1820. Carpenter, residing in Baltimore, Maryland. 14 February 1852.

Lynde, Richard D. M. D.: Born 8 July 1830, Fort Machinack, Michigan. U. S. Army Physician. Married. 15 September 1856.

Mackale, Richard G.: Born 9 November 1809, Calvert County, Maryland. Resides in Calvert County, Maryland. Farmer. 5 July 1848.

Maddox, John H.: Born 28 November 1807, Charles County, Maryland. Resides in Fredericksburg, Virginia. Food Merchant, Going into Timber business. 26 June 1835.

Magahey, James O. Born 8 August 1825, Bond County, Mississippi. Resides in Bond Co., Mississippi. Going to California. 7 April 1849.

Magahey, James S.: Born 14 September 1836, Greenville, Illinois. Resides in Greenville, Illinois. Carpenter. Going to California. 7 April 1849.

Magruder, John B: Born in Caroline County, Virginia 1 May 1807. Resides in Baltimore, Maryland. U. S. Army Artillery officer. 17 February 1834.

Major, 16: Born Hanover Co., Va. Employed in brickyard. Insured by Thomas Pollard for John Henry Wickham.

Mann, Joseph: Born November 1797, Worcester, Massachusetts. Resides in Fredericksburg, Virginia. Confectioner. 7 July 1838.

Manor, Elizabeth: Born in Pennsylvania, 1802. Resides in Jay County, Indiana. Insured by William D. Daniel, Berkeley County, Va. (Winchester). 12 January 1837.

Baltimore Life Insurance Company Applications

Marean, Silas: Born 1780, Masachusetts. Resides in Baltimore, Maryland. Merchant. Original application 12 October 1831. Policy renewed 1 September 1835.

Maria: Born in Baltimore, Maryland May 1819. Resides in Baltimore, Md. Slave employed as a house servant. Insured by Nicholas Brewer 2 June 1834.

Marr, James H.: Born near Port Tobacco, Charles Co., Md. 4 November 1810. Residence Washington, D. C. Postal clerk. 20 February 1851.

Marshall, Alexander John: Born in Warrenton, Fauquier County, Virginia. Clerk of the County Court of Fauquier County. 15 January 1836.

Marshall, Polly, 38: Born Richmond, Va. Residence in Richmond. Cook, married. Slave insured by Louisa Carrington.

Marshall, Thomas F: Born at Frankford, Kentucky 7 June 1801. Resides in Woodford County, Kentucky. Lawyer, member of Congress of the United States (10th. District, Kentucky). 5 March 1842.

Martha Ann, 12: Born Hanover Co.,Va. Residence Richmond,Va. Employed as a house servant. Insured by William M. Sutton for Thomas Doswell.

Martin, Anderson: Born 5 March 1808, Kentucky. Resides in Richmond, Missouri. 7 March 1849.

Masi, Serapheim: Born 11 July 1799, Italy. Resides in Washington, D. C. Jewelry dealer. 28 February 1834.

Mason, Hester: B Accomack County, Virginia. Age between 44 and 46. Housewife. William Mason, spouse. 25 February 1852.

Mason, J. Thompson: Born 20 March 1818, Loudon County, Virginia. Naval surgeon, residing in Baltimore, Maryland. 31 May 1852.

Mason, Sarah Catherine: Born 4 March 1820, St. Mary's County, Maryland. Resides in St. Augustine, Florida. 1 May 1849.

Baltimore Life Insurance Company
Applications

Matlock, Richard C.: Born September 1810,
Culpepper County, Virginia. Resides in Baltimore,
Maryland. Salesman. Insured by F. Gardner. 12
January 1849.
Matthews, William Jesse: Born in Lower Marlboro,
Calvert Co., Maryland. Free Negro. Resides in
Baltimore, Maryland. Employed as waiter & white
washer. 13 March 1841.
Maulsby, William P.: Born 10 July 1815, Bel Air,
Hartford County, Maryland. Resides Baltimore,
Maryland. Lawyer. 6 July 1850.
Maxey, Virgil: Born in Massachusetts, 5 May 1784.
Resides in Washington, D. C. Solicitor of the
Treasury. 17 November 1834.
Maxey/Maxcy, Virgil: Born in Eastern U. S. Resides
in Washington, D. C. Charge d'Affairs to Brussels.
Insured by Martin Fennick & John C. Means 28
February 1828.
Mayer, Charles F: of Lewis: Born in Philadelphia,
Pa. 1826. Merchant, residing in Baltimore. 27 July
1857
McAllister, Robert: Born 18 August 1816,
Baltimore, Maryland. Resides in Baltimore,
Maryland @ 184 Wolfe Street. Shipping Master.
McClellan, David W. B.: Born 21 March 1797,
Adams County, Pennsylvania. Resides in Baltimore,
Maryland. Physician. 18 July 1835.
McClellan, Samuel: Born 1787. Resides in
Baltimore, Maryland. 24 October 1834.
McClellan, William: Born 27 March 1817. Resides
in Baltimore, Md. Gentleman. December 1851.
McCollum, Elizabeth, 44: Born Frederick Co., Md.
Oct 1812. Residence in Baltimore. Housewife,
insured by John McCollum. 30 August 1859.
McCollum, John 49: Born Lancaster Co., Pa. 20
July 1807. Resides "at the almshouse, where I am
overseer'. 13 May 1856.
McColm, Edward M: Born 7 October 1809,
Baltimore, Md. Resides in Baltimore, Md. Speculator
in firewood. 15 November 1836.

Baltimore Life Insurance Company Applications

McConnell, Edward: Born in Wilmington, Delaware. Resides in Richmond, Virginia. Elizabeth McConnell, spouse. 18 September 1834.

McCormick, Hugh: Born 15 June 1801, Washington, D. C. Resides in Washington, D. C. Teacher at the Eastern ___ School, Washington, D. C. 24 October 1835.

McCormick, James: Born 31 January 1816, Montgomery County, Ohio (near Dayton). Resides in Cincinnati, Ohio. Seaman in U. S. Navy going to the East Indies on Frigate *Columbia.* 20 December 1837.

McCullough, William: Born Cecil Co., Md. 29 June 1808. Residence Annapolis, Md. 2 January 1850.

McDonald, Grace: Born in Baltimore, Md. 6 August 1795. Resides in Baltimore, Md. 6 August 1836.

McDonald, Michael: Born in Anne Arundel County, Maryland. Age 49. Resides in Baltimore, Maryland. Captain of the Brig "Amazon". 26 August 1849.

McGee, J. W: 6 May 1837. Age 36, Born Billifont Center Co, Pa. 25 April 1821. Resides in Warrenton, Va., dentist.

McGee, M. A: Insures two Negroes employed in Richmond at Tobacco Factory. **Spencer, age 28,** Born Hanover Co, Va; **Anderson, 19,** Born Hanover Co, Va. 15 September 1855.

McGehee, Lewis: Born 6 February 1821, Tuscaloosa, Alabama. Resides in Washington, D. C. Clerk. **McGinnis, Francis I:** Born Baltimore, Maryland 12 January 1812. Clerk for Fireman's Assurance Association, residing in Baltimore, Maryland. 11 June 1852.

McGuire, Hugh H: Born in Frederick County, Virginia 6 November 1861. Resides in Winchester, Virginia. Physician. 28 November 1835.

McIntosh, James. Insured 25 November 1841. Employed in U. S. Navy.

McInTosh, James: 25 Nov. 1841. U. S. Navy.

McKean, H. Pratt: Born 5 May 1810, Philadelphia, Pennsylvania, Resides in Philadelphia, Pennsylvania. Merchant. 5 November 1838.

Baltimore Life Insurance Company Applications

McKee, John: Born January 1821, Ireland. Resides in Baltimore, Maryland. Supercargo. Spouse is Esther Jane McKee.

McKeever, Isaac: Born in Pennsylvania. Age 40. Captain in U. S. Navy. 3 October 1842.

McKenney, William: Born in Maryland 23 April 1790. Resides in Baltimore, Maryland. Minister. Age 47.

McLane, Allen: Born 8 June 1823, Wilmington, Delaware. U. S. Navy officer on the steamer 'California'. 13 July 1849.

McLaughlin, Augustus: Born Baltimore, Maryland 18 January 1823. Midshipman, assigned to the Mediterranean Fleet of the U. S. Navy.

McLaughlin, William: Born 20 December 1803, Havre de Grace, Maryland. Resides in Baltimore, Maryland. Lottery Broker. 5 June 1849.

McLean, Cornelius: Born 15 March 1807, Bladensburg, Maryland. Resides in Annapolis, Maryland. Attorney, Chancellor of the Maryland Land Office. 8 August 1850.

McNeir, George Jr.: Born 6 February 1824, Maryland. Resides in Washington, D. C. 8 February 1850.

McNeir, George: Born in Annapolis, Maryland 28 May 1794. Resides in Annapolis. Port Master.

McPherson, John: Born 16 April 1796, Frederick County, Maryland. Resides Urbana, Frederick County, Maryland. Baltimore City Flour Inspector. 14 July 1849.

McTyre, Thomas, 36: Born Chesterfield Co., Va. Slave, employed at Black Heath Coal Pits. Insured by Theodore Tompkins for R. M. Mctyre.

Meade, Holmes: Born 1 May 1796, Rutland, Vermont. Resides in Granville, Ohio. Farmer. Insured by Samuel Vance 31 May 1850.

Meade, Richard W: Born Cadiz, Spain, 21 March 1807. Resides in New York. Lieutenant in U. S. Navy. 29 March 1839.

Baltimore Life Insurance Company Applications

Medcalfe, Charles: Born 3 November 1823, Baltimore, Maryland. Resides in Baltimore, Md. Merchant. Married. Henrietta M. Medcalfe, spouse.

Meeds, John Davis: Born May 1821, Maryland. Resides in Baltimore, Maryland. Clerk. Luther I. Cox, beneficiary. 9 March 1841.

Mele, Frances: Born 21 August 1822, Germany. Resides in Zanesville, Ohio. Baker. 27 March 1850.

Mercer, William F.: Born March 1815, Howard District, Maryland. Resides at Ellicott's Mills, Maryland Going to California. 31 August 1849.

Meriwether, William: Born 15 May 1796, Jefferson County, Kentucky. Resides in Louisville, Kentucky. Physician. 22 February 1836.

Merker, Andrew: Born in Alsace, France 10 February 1804. Resides in Baltimore, Maryland. White Smith. 5 January 1835.

Merriken, James: Born 4 November 1785, Baltimore, Maryland. Resides at Baltimore, Md. Cabinetmaker and Sexton, St. Paul's Church. 3 January 1834.

Merryman, Samuel W: Born 26 November 1806, Baltimore County, Maryland. Resides in Baltimore, Maryland @ # 8 Market Place. Dry Goods merchant. 33 November 1838.

Micows, William: Born in Augusta Georgia 14 January 1807. Resides in Augusta, Georgia. Attorney and Post Master. 14 September 1835.

Middleton, Reuben: Born 27 January 1814. Residence in St. Joseph's, Missouri. 7 March 1849.

Middleton, William G.: Born in Baltimore, Maryland. Age 30. resides in Baltimore, Maryland. Engaged in the Dry Goods business. 7 March 1850.

Miley: Born in St. Mary's Co., Md. Age 27. Cooper at Tobacco warehouse. Insured by William Reeder. 29 December 1836.

Milhausen, Henry B: B 27 January 1825, Germany. Working on the Pacific Railroad Survey. 30 May 1853.

Baltimore Life Insurance Company Applications

Miller, Edwin A.: Born 28 May 1828, Harford County, Maryland. Resides in Baltimore, Maryland. In the 'Notion ' business. 18 December 1848.

Mills, Enoch G.: Born 1 September 1817 in Calvert Co. Md. Residence in Calvert Co, Md. Farmer. 23 June 1851.

Minerva, age 29 Born Goochland County, Va. J. P. Talley, Richmond, Va.

Minifie, William: Born 14 August 1805, Devonshire, England. Bookseller and Stationeer, residing in Baltimore, Maryland. 17 July 1845.

Minor, George: Born Fredericksburg, Va. 12 May 1808. Lieutenant, U. S. Navy assigned to U. S Warren, Pacific Theater. 3 October 1843.

Mitchel: 16 Oct. 1855. A slave belonging to William R. Trent of Henrico Co., Va. Claim paid 17 October 1857.

Mitchell, age 35, Born Henrico, Va., Coal Pit hand in Henrico Co, Va., Married. William R. Trent Insurer.

Mitchell, Alexander: Born in 1776. Resides in Baltimore , Maryland. Manufacturer. Insured by Charles F. Mayer. 6 August 1832.

Mitchell, Elizabeth: Born 11 July 1773, Baltimore, Maryland. Resides in Baltimore, Maryland on Front Street opposite Christ Church. Housewife insured by Alexander Mitchell. 19 January 1835.

Mitchell. A slave belonging to William R. Trent of Henrico Co., Va. Insured 16 October 1855. Claim paid 17 October 1857.

Montell, Francis: Born March 1811. Location illegible. Resides in Baltimore, Maryland. Merchant. 22 December 1837.

Montgomery, Alexander: Born 11 April 1826, Philadelphia, Pennsylvania. Resides in St. Louis, Missouri. Going to California. 14 April 1849.

Montgomery, Robert G: Born 22 February 1813, Westmoreland County, Virginia. Resides in Richmond County, Virginia. Teacher and Farmer. Insured by Augusta Neale, guardian of George Born A. McCarty 28 January 1842.

Baltimore Life Insurance Company Applications

Moody, Theodore L.: Born State of Maine 30 June 1804. Residence in Washington, D. C. Employed at U. S. Treasury Department. 16 April 1851.

Moore, Alfred L: Born 20 August 1802, Baltimore, Maryland. Resides in Baltimore, Maryland. Mercantile businessman. Father was a physician. Planning to travel to Texas during the fall & winter of 1841. 19 December 1840.

Moore, Edward W: Born July 1810. U. S. Navy officer. 18 March 1836.

Moore, P. T: Born 22 September 1822 in Ireland. Residence in Richmond, Va. Hardware business. 6 October 1851.

Moore, Thomas J.: B 18 December 1820 in Charles Co., Md. Residence in Lexington, Fayette Co., Kentucky. Dealer in Marble.

Mordicai, Sam: Born 24 July 1786, New York. Resides in Petersburg, Virginia. Merchant. 10 April 1839.

Morell, William H.: Born Lenox, Massachusetts 9 March 1800. Resides in Winchester, Virginia. Civil Engineer. 6 October 1835.

Morgan, C. C: Born in New York. Age about 37. Resides in Lancaster Ohio. Canal boat captain employed and insured by Perry Smith & co. 28 March 1850.

Morgan, Charles W: Born in Virgina. Age 53. Commander of the Mediterranean Squadron of the U. S. Navy. Insured by Andrew McLaughlin 4 September 1841.

Morrell, Joshua: Born September 1815, Calvert Co., Md. Resides West River, A. A. Co. Md. Episcopal clergyman. 2 December 1856

Morrison, Samuel A.: Born 20 June 1818, Peterborough, New Hampshire. Resides in Baltimore, Maryland. Engaged in 'commerce'. 20 June 1847.

Morson, Arthur A.: Born 17 September 1849, Stafford County, Virginia. Resides in Richmond, Virginia. Lawyer. 17 September 1849.

Baltimore Life Insurance Company Applications

Mosby, Edward C: Born 10 June 1802, Powhaten County, Virginia. Resides Jefferson, Powhatan County, Virginia. County Sheriff. 4 September 1838.
Mosby, Littleberry H: Born 1 September 1789, Powhaten County, Virginia. Resides in Louisville, Kentucky. Physician. 26 January 1836.
Mosby, William W.: Born 20 June 1800, Powhatten County, Virginia. Grain dealer residing in Lynchburg, Virginia. Has two children, Charles L. and Betsy H. 1 July 1850.
Moses: Age 12. Age 30. Valued at $600. slave being transported to Savannah, Georgia. Insured by James H. Hammond.
Moulton, Ferdinand: Born 26 September 1824, Carroll County, New Hampshire. Lawyer, residing in Washington, D. C. 8 August 1853.
Mulhausen, Henrich B: Born 27 January 1825, Germany. Pacific Railroad Survey Party member. 30 May 1853.
Muller, August: Born in Germany, February, 1812. A laborer at Mt. Claire Railroad Station, residing in Baltimore, Maryland.
Munn, Samuel E: 29 Dec. 1842.
Murphy, Thomas S: Born in Baltimore, Maryland 15 September 1798. Resides in Baltimore. Shipmaster, employed by William Wilson & Sons. 7 July 1842.
Murphy, Thomas: Born 16 September 1798. Letter requesting insurance give no other data. 1 July 1835.
Murray, Henry Negro, 48: Born Anne Arundel Co. March 1808. Coachman. Residence in Baltimore with Joseph C. Wilson, 7 July 1856.
Murray, James: Born April 1786/1787 in Annapolis, Maryland. Going to Wisconsin as Indian Commissioner under the Treaty of 1837. 9 August 1838.
Murray, John: Born in Ireland. Age about 37. A shoe dealer, residing in Baltimore, Maryland. 29 January 1849.

Baltimore Life Insurance Company Applications

Murray, Samuel: slave of James Brimm. Born Kent Co., Md. Resides in Queen Ann's Co., Md. Farmhand. 1 April 1857.

Muse, William T.. Insured 11 March 1844.

Nat: A slave Born in Calvert County, Maryland. Insured by Edward Reynolds 13 August 1850.

Nathan: 13 January 1852. ($500) Insured. Claim Paid 18 January 1856.

Neal, Joseph: Born in Baltimore, Maryland 8 January 1805. Resides in Baltimore, Maryland. Trader.

Nearman, Charles: Born 5 July 1830, Germany. Resides in Baltimore, Maryland. Laborer at B & O Railroad. (Mt Clare Station). 25 March 1856.

Nelson, 14: Born Nelson Co., Va. Residence in Richmond, Va. Employed as tobacco factory hand. Slave. Insured by Dr. R. T. Coleman.

Nelson, 40: Slave employed in Tobacco factory. Residence in Richmond, Va. Insured by J. H. T. Mayo.

Newell, Lloyd B: 11 August 1842. Francis Johnson of Baltimore, beneficiary. 21 May 1857.

Newell, Lloyd R: Born in Washington, Georgia 18 February 1804. Resides in Washington, D. C. U. S. Navy Lieutenant. 17 May 1836 (at Norfolk, Virginia).

Nicholson, August A: Born in Charleston, South Carolina. Resides in Philadelphia, Pennsylvania. U. S. Marine Captain.

Nollner, Jacob: Born 1 August 1799, Orange County, North Carolina. Resides in Washington, D. C. Clerk in the General Land Office. 26 June 1835.

Norman, Samuel: Born near West River, Annapolis, Maryland, 1789. Resides near West River. Farmer. 13 October 1842.

Norris, John Lauren: Born 25 March 1813 in Baltimore, Md. Residence in Baltimore. Assistant Treasurer of Savings Bank of Baltimore. 9 June 1851.

Baltimore Life Insurance Company Applications

Nutwell, John L. E.: Born April 1810, Anne Arundel county, Maryland. Farmer, residing in Anne Arundel County, Maryland. 16 January 1850.

Oden, George: Machinist, Born in Rappahannock, Virginia, age 25. Resides in Front Royal Virginia. 2 September 1852.

Odersley, Harriet: Age 40, resides in Baltimore, Maryland. 13 July 1835.

Ogden, William L.: Born 1805/06, New York. U. S. Navy Officer. 7 August 1834, 16 August 1838..

Ogle, Atkin S: Born in Yorkshire, England 6 November 1797. Resides in Baltimore County, Maryland. Planning an extended visit to Petersburg, Va. Builder of houses. Not dated.

Oleria, age 13: Richard F. Danacott, insurer.

Osbourne, Charles F: Born 25 December 1800. Resides at Petersburg, Virginia. President of the Petersburg R. R. Co. January 1839.

Ould Robert: Born in Georgetown, D. C. 31 January 1820. Residence in Georgetown, D. C. Attorney at Law. 10 May 1851.

Owen, John: Born Montgomery Shire, North Wales 22 May 1804. Resides in Kent County, Maryland. Farmer. 16 January 1850.

Page, Charles: age 14, Born Hanover County, Va, 6 January 1834. Benjamin Pollard

Pairo, Charles W: Born 24 July 1810, Washington, D. C. Resides in Washington, D. C. Banker. 4 September 1850.

Palmer, Harriet: Born 31 March 1794, New Jersey. Resides in Baltimore, Maryland. 8 March 1848.

Palmer, Harriet: Born Burlington, N. J. 1794. Residence in Baltimore, Md. 24 November 1849.

Palmer, Harriet: Born in Philadelphia, Pennsylvania. Age about 45-50. Resides in Baltimore, Maryland. 10 January 1845.

Palmer, Thomas: Born 20 December 1791, New York. Resides in Baltimore, Maryland. Voyaging to Europe. Harriet Palmer, spouse. 28 January 1834.

Baltimore Life Insurance Company Applications

Parish, John G.: Born In Fredericksburg, Virginia 23 December 1817. Resides in Bowling Green, Virginia. Merchant. 2 March 1849.

Parker, Foxhall A: Born 1790 in Westmoreland County, Virginia. Resides at Norfolk, Virginia. U. S. Navy Captain. 20 February 1838.

Parker, Mrs. Ellen E.: Born in 1817 or 1818. Location not stated. Residence in Baltimore, Maryland. Housekeeper. Has children. Insured by Edward O. Hinkley. 19 November 1851.

Parrish, John G.: Born 23 December 1817 in Frederickburg, Va. Residence in Bowling Green, Va. Minister.

Patterson, Carlisle S: Born in St. Louis, Missouri, 16 August 1816. Resides in Washington, D. C. U. S. Navy. 2 January 1837.

Patterson, Daniel T: Born 10 March 1785, New York. Resides in the District of Columbia. Commandant, US. Naval Yard. 3 November 1837.

Paul: Slave of M's Elizabeth F. Gilliam, Richmond, Va. Insured 8 February 1858.

Payne, William W: Born in Front Royal Virginia 20 April 1797. Resides in Washington, D. C. Postal clerk. 6 July 1835.

Peabody, Adolphus W: Born in Georgetown, D. C. 13 October 1814. Resides in Georgetown, D. C. Plans to go to California. 1 February 1849.

Peebles, C. G. Born 3 July 1807. Resides in Washington, D. C. Clerk. 25 July 1849.

Pendleton, John S: Born 1 March 1802, Culpeper County, Virgina. Resides in Culpepper County, Virginia. Attorney. Charge d"Affairs of the United States to Chile. 15 December 1841.

Perine, E. Glenn: Born 14 June 1829, Baltimore, Md. Resides in Baltimore, Md. Flour maker. 17 July 1855.

Baltimore Life Insurance Company Applications

Perry: Slave insured by L. Hilliary: in possession of Jacob Fechtig, to indemnify Joseph Everstine against personal losses in administration of the estate of Margaret Hilliary. 25 October 1834. Cumberland, Maryland.

Peter, 15: Born Chesterfield Co., Va. Slave, employed at Black Heath Coal Pits. Insured by Theodore Tompkins for William E. Martin.

Peter, 25: Born Norththumberland Co., Va. Slave, farmhand. Insured by T. L. D. Covington.

Peter, a slave: Born Hanover County, Va. age 22, employed on the Danville R.R. 6 January 1834.. Application of Ella F. Temple of Richmond, Va.

Peter: Born 13 February 1832, Hanover County, Virginia. Slave, residing in Richmond, Va. Employed as a brick maker by Peter D. Ginn. 30 February 1852.

Peter: Born Hanover Co. Va. Age about 45. Slave employed by James Dunlop to work in coal or coke pits in Hanover Co. Va. Insured by Lucian. Born Price of Hanover Co., Va. 21 August 1855.

Peter: slave of L. B. Price. Born Hanover Co., Va. 1807. Resides in Henrico Co., Va. Laborer.

Peter: Slave, Born and residing in Howard County, Maryland. Age 46. Employed as a farmhand by Edward T. Ellicott. Insured by W. Summerville. 5 September 1852.

Peterkin, Joshua: Born 2 August 1814, Baltimore, Maryland. Resides in Frederick County, Maryland. Schoolmaster. 28 September 1849.

Peters, Jesse T: Stockbroker, Born in Baltimore, Maryland 30 September 1800. Resides in Baltimore, Maryland. 12 December 1852.

Pettrich, Ferdinand: Born Dresden, Germany 9 December 1798. Resides in Washington, D. C. Sculptor. 11 September 1838.

Peyton: Age about 48. Slave of George Whitlock. Tobacconist, age 48. Resides in Richmond, Va.

Phenix, Thomas: Born Prince George's Co., Md. 16 Nov 1791.Resides in Baltimore, Md. Cashier of the Western Bank. 1 February 1837.

Baltimore Life Insurance Company Applications

Phil: Born 4 January 1834. D. Lee Powell, insurer, Hanover County, Va. Resides in Richmond,. Employed on Danville R.R.

Phillip, age 55: Born Powhatten, Va. Laborer in Richmond. Ann C. Darracote, Richmond, Va.

Pinkney, Henry: U. S. Navy.[3]

Piper, James: No data given. Application is a letter from A. Goldner, requesting insurance, dated 16 December 1834.

Plant, James K.: Born April 1801, Manchester, England. Resides in Washington, D. C. Cabinetmaker.

Pleasants, Benjamin F: Born in Goochland County, Virginia 10 November 1795. Resides in Washington, D. C. Clerk in the office of the Solicitor of the Treasury. 2 February 1835.

Pleasants, Charles E. Rev.: Born 9 December 1801, Philadelphia, Pennsylvania. Resides in Lewistown, Delaware. Minister. 4 February 1836.

Plitt, Charles: Born in Pennsylvania 17 October 1809. Resides in Washington, D. C. Post Office clerk. 20 May 1836.

Plowman, Eli R: Born 30 January 1805, York County, Pennsylvania. Resides in Baltimore, Maryland. Confectioner. 2 November 1841.

Plympton, William: Born in Massachusetts in 1793. A merchant in New York, N. Y. Insured by Daniel Boyd 27 October 1836.

Poe, Nelson: Born in Baltimore, Maryland 11 August 1809. Resides in Baltimore. Newspaper publisher. Wife: Josephine Poe. 26 June 1838.

Poindexter, T. B: Planter, Born in Virginia 15 Age about 50. Resides in Louisiana. 15 December 1852.

Porter, Henry: Born 26 January 1793, Philadelphia, Pennsylvania. Shovel manufacturer, residing in Baltimore, Maryland. 4 April 1853.

---

[3] No application in folder. Receipt for premiums only.

Baltimore Life Insurance Company Applications

Posey, Benjamin: Age about 28. Slave, employed as a servant by N. Ross. Owned by James C____. 13 February 1852.

Potter, Zabdiel: Born 22 December 1813, Caroline County, Maryland. Resides in Caroline County, Maryland. US. Consul to Chile. 6 November 1849. .

Prather, Henrietta M: Born 10 July 1814 in Washington, D. C. Resides in Washington, D. C. Seamstress. 18 January 1836.

Prentiss, John: Born 1799, Massachusetts. Resides in Baltimore, Maryland, teacher. 23 May 1840.

Prentiss, William: Born 23 October 1797 in Washington, D. C. Resides in Washington, D. C. Distributor of Laws for the U. S. State Department. 8 October 1835.

Preston, Charles F: Born 3 April 1816, Northbridge, Massachusetts. Resides in Savannah, Georgia. Bookkeeper.

Preston, Robert J.: Born in Ireland, July 1811. Resides in Augusta, Kentucky. Merchant. 23 April 1850.

Prevost, Lewis M.: Born 20 March 1818, Philadelphia, Pennsylvania. Resides in Spotsylvania County, Virginia. Civil Engineer. 21 January 1849.

Price, A. M: Born 7 June 1800, Cecil County, Maryland. Resides in Baltimore, Maryland. Grocer. 22 October 1835.

Price, John: Born in England. Resides in Clinton, Mississippi. Land Office Clerk. Insured by William M. Gouge. 2 July 1835.

Price, Thomas: Born 14 May 1807, Herefordshire, England. Resides in Zanesville, Ohio. Foundry fireman. 16 January 1850.

Prout, Sarah E.: Born in Anne Arundel County, Maryland. Age about 33 –35. Resides in Calvert County, Maryland. Housewife. 22 February 1849.

Quissonberry, William: Born 20 May 1797, Caroline County, Virginia. Resides in Caroline County, Virginia. Mail contractor. 18 March 1836.

Baltimore Life Insurance Company Applications

Ragan, Danice: Born 8 September 1802, Loudon County, Virginia. Resides at Georgetown, D. C. Removing to St. Louis, Missouri (U. S. Arsenal). Military Store Keeper.

Ragsdale, Anna Maria McLean, Born Petersburg, Virginia 1802, residence Tarboro, N.C. 24 December 1838.

Ragsdale, Susan Eliza: Born 1805, Petersburg, Virginia. Resides at Tarboro, North Carolina. 1 January 1839.

Ragsdale, Thomas L: Born in Orange County, North Carolina 1 March 1798. Resides in Washington, D. C. U. S. Navy Department clerk. 16 June 1835.

Raisin, Horace: Slave, residing in Kent County, Maryland. Age about 15/16. insured by George Preyman, Baltimore, Maryland 20 February 1853.

Ralph, age 20: Porter to Powhatan House. Richmond, Va. Richard F. Danacott, insurer.

Ramsey, Charles R: Born in New Jersey, 27 January 1806. Resides in Washington, D. C. Post Office clerk. 1 December 1834.

Ramsey, William. Born Alexandria, Va. Residence in Washington, D. C. Naval Officer. 21 July 1835.

Ramsey, William: Born. Alexandria , Va. Resides in Washington, D. C. A naval officer. Application date 21 July 1835.

Ramsey, Wordsworth: Born 1824, Georgetown, District of Columbia. Resides in St. Louis, Missouri.

Randolph, G. W.: Born 10 March 1818, Albermarle County, Virginia. Student at the University of Virginia. 5 August 1839.

Redd, John: Born Hanover, Va. Age 26. A slave hired out to work on the Danville Railroad. Insured by D. Lee Powell. 4 January 1834.

Reeder, William A: Born in St. Mary's County, Maryland August 1820. Resides in Burlington Territory, Iowa. Physician. 22 May 1841.

Reese, John E: Born at Baltimore, Maryland April 1798. Resides in Baltimore, Maryland. Clerk in the Planter;s & Farmers Bank. 26 February 1839.

Baltimore Life Insurance Company Applications

Reich, Phillip: Born in Frederick, Maryland 7 November 1797. Resides in Frederick, Maryland. Farmer. 17 August 1835.

Reinhardt, Henry: Born Germany 23 March 1815. Residence in Baltimore. Removing to Charleston, S. C. Instrument maker. 14 November 1850.

Retan, Samuel J: Born 6 July 1850, Connecticut. Millwright, residing in Baltimore, Maryland. 22 July 1850.

Reuben, age 45: Born Hanover County, Va. Resides in Richmond. 6 January 1834. Mary Thornton, Richmond, Va.

Reuben. A slave insured by Thomas W. Doswell, Richmond, Va. Trustee of William P. H. Davenport.

Reuben: Slave of George Whitlock. Laborer, age 50. Resides in Richmond, Va.

Ricards, John Robert: Born 5 October 1804, Sussex County, Delaware. Resides in Baltimore, Maryland. Dry Goods Merchant. 7 September 1841.

Rice, Francis A: Born 4 September 1810, Logan County, Kentucky. Medical student in Louisville, Kentucky. 18 December 1840.

Richard, 20: lives somewhere on the line of the R.R. 6 January 1834. Benjamin Pollard, insurer.

Richard, 24: Born Chesterfield, Va. Slave, employed at Black Heath Coal Pits. Insured by Theodore Tompkins for William E. Martin.

Richard. Slave of Edward M. Henry, Fredericksburg, Va. Insured 24 August 1855.

Richard., a slave. Age about 33: Born King & Queen Co., Va. Resides in Richmond, Va. Employed at Tobacco Factory. Insured by E. M. Henry, owner.

Richard: 24 August 1855, Slave of Edward M. Henry of Fredricksburg, Va.

Richard: A slave Born in Calvert County, Maryland. Insured by Edward Reynolds 13 August 1850.

Richards, Adolph: Born 10 October 1805, Curacao, West Indies. Resides at Fredericksburg, Virginia. Painter, Turner, Chair & bed maker. 11 December 1838.

Baltimore Life Insurance Company Applications

Richards, John C: Born 1 June 1812, Baltimore, Maryland. Physician. Spouse, Elizabeth Born in Harford County, Maryland 11 May 1814. Residence in Baltimore. 26 December 1834.

Richardson, Edward D: Surveyor Born and residing in Harford County, Maryland. Birth date 28 May 1810. 7 January 1853.

Richardson, Edward J: Born in Baltimore, Md. Age about 36. Resides in Baltimore, in mercantile business.

Richardson, George R.: Born 6 August 1801, Worcester County, Maryland. Resides in Baltimore, Maryland. Lawyer. 2 May 1836.

Richardson, George W: Born in Baltimore, Maryland April 1803. Resides at Baltimore, Maryland. Businessman. 16 February 1839.

Richardson, George: Born in Baltimore, Maryland in March 1805. Resides in Baltimore. Merchant. 15 November 1842.

Riddle, Robert: Born 17 August 1812, Pittsburgh, Pennsylvania. Resides in Philadelphia, Pa. Merchant. 23 January 1837.

Ridgaway, William: Born 6 July 1784, Easton, Md. Resides in Baltimore, Md. (Water St.) Tailor. 18 April 1838.

Ridgely, Charles L: Born in Baltimore, Maryland 3 June 1811. Resides in Ann Arundel County, Maryland. U. S. Naval Officer. 28 April 1836.

Ridgely, James P.: Born 21 November 1818, Elkridge, Maryland. Resides in Baltimore, Maryland. U. S. Army Officer. 7 July 1850.

Ridgely, James: Born 21 November 1818, Anne Arundel county, Maryland. Resides in Baltimore, Maryland. U. S. Navy. 12 December 1848.

Ridgely, Mary: Born in Prince George's County, Maryland 9 February 1784. Resides in Baltimore, Md. # 15 Baltimore Street. Housewife. Spouse Lote Ridgely. 24 July 1833.

Baltimore Life Insurance Company Applications

Ridgely, Richard H. L.: Born 21 December 1830 in Baltimore, Md. Residence in Baltimore, Md. Is not employed. 29 July 1850.

Riley, John: Born 19 September 1851 in Harrison co, Ohio. Residence in Zanesville, Ohio. Employed as a traveling agent. Insured by William F. Kent. 14 November 1850.

Ringgold, Cadusladu: Born in Washington Co, Maryland. Resides in Baltimore, Md. Lieutenant, U. S. Navy. 24 June 1834.

Ritchie, William B: Born in Scotland, 13 October 1794. Resides at Petersburg, Va. Clerk. 18 February 1839.

Rittenhouse, F: Born 7 August 1805 in Northumberland Co., Pennsylvania. Residence in Alexandria Co., Va. 4 miles from the U. S. Treasury Dept. Clerk at U. S. Treasury. 18 June 1851.

Rittenhouse, John B: 44: Born Georgetown, D. C. 14 June 1872. U. S. Navy Purser, Benefits payable to Charles E. Rittenhouse, trustee.

Roane, William: Born 8 May 1824, Amherst County, Virginia. Resides in Lynchburg, Virginia. Attorney at Law. 19 July 1849.

Robbins, Julius A.: Born May 1821, Connecticut. Resides in Goliad, Texas. Engaged in merchandising. Insured by H. W. Robbins, Baltimore, Maryland 19 January 1849.

Robert, 41: Born Prince Edward Co., Va. Slave, employed at Black Heath Coal Pits. Insured by Theodore Tompkins for William E. Martin.

Robert. Age about 39: Born King & Queen Co., Va. Resides & is employed at Tobacco Factory in Richmond, Va. Insured by E. M. Henry, owner.

Robert. Slave of Edward M. Henry, Fredericksburg, Va. Insured 24 August 1855.

Robert: Born in Henrico Co., Va. Age about 27. Slave, employed in a tobacco factory. Insured by Elizabeth M. Binford 11 August 1857.

Baltimore Life Insurance Company Applications

Roberts, Christiana G.: Born 22 January 1837 in Northampton Co., Va. Residence in Baltimore, Maryland. A student at the Baltimore Female College. Insured by George E. Bowdin, agent for James W. Custis. 22 April 1851.

Robertson, Maria M: Born 28 December 1802, Chesterfield County, Virginia. Resides in Chesterfield Co., Va. Housewife. John T. Robertson insurer and spouse. 15 April 1834.

Robertson, Thomas: Born in Norfolk County, Virginia 1793. Resides in Norfolk, Virginia. Teller at the Farmers Bank. 3 May 1836.

Robinson William, Jr:. Born Augusta, Maine June 1805. Residence in Baltimore since 1820, supercargo. 30 September 1831.

Robinson, George, 46: Born Fauquier Co, Va. Residence Henrico Co., Va. Employed as farmhand. 14 February 1857.

Robinson, John: Born in Maryland30 March 1797. Resides in Washington, D. C. Watchman at U. S. Department of War. 1 December 1836.

Rodewald, Henry: Born in Germany, age 38. resides in Baltimore. 20 February 1835.

Rogers, Eliza: Born 6 miles north. of Baltimore City, age 18. Slave in household of Mrs. Thomas Kelso, East Baltimore. Street, Baltimore, Maryland.

Rogers, Gilbert Jr.: Born 27 November 1813, Groton, Conn. Accountant residing in Baltimore, Md. 4 February 1852.

Rogers, John Jr.: Born Philadelphia February 4 1820, resides #26 Pine St., employed as clerk in Baltimore. Spouse is Susan Rogers. 27 January 1859.

Rooker, Jabez Berry: Born 3 April 1792, Wahall, Staffordshire County, England. Resides in Washington, D. C. chief Clerk or the Office of the Commissioner of Public Buildings. 23 August 1838.

Rosa: Age 20. Valued at $800. Slave being transported to Savannah, Georgia. Insured by James H. Hammond.

Baltimore Life Insurance Company Applications

Rosenthal, Augusta Sophia: Born 26 January 1805, Leidenbuch, Germany. Resides in Georgetown, D. C. Spouse is Charles. Housewife. 19 September 1848.

Rosenthal, Charles, G. E.: Born 17 July 1804, Berlin , Germany. Resides in Georgetown, D. C. Refectory Keeper. 19 September 1848.

Ross, John: Born 16 April 1789, Scotland. Resides in Wright County, Virginia. Farmer. 1 December 1837.

Ross, Richard H: Born 13 March 1806, Bladensburg, Maryland. Resides in Baton Rouge, Louisiana. U. S. Army Captain. 16 November 1848.

Ross, Robert T: Salesman, Born 16 March 1820, Bladensburg, Maryland. Resides in Baltimore, Maryland. 14 March 1853.

Rothreck, Larkin J: Born 18 March 1831. Going to California. 29 March 1849.

Rowe, Dexter: Born Sunderland, Massachusetts, 21 August 1825. Resides in Baltimore, Maryland. Engaged in the mercantile business. 13 June 18149.

Roy, A. T, 28: Born Fredericksburg, Va. 29 October 1829. Residence in Fredericksburg, Va. Unemployed. 2 March 1857.

Royall, John M: Born in Powhatten County, Virginia 11 September 1814. Resides in Richmond, Va. Merchant. Beneficiary is wife, Isabella Royall. 8 November 1836.

Ruckle, John: Born in Baltimore, Maryland September 1804. Resides in Baltimore. Employed by Tiffany Ward & Co. 8 November 1842.

Rudenstein, John: Born Baltimore, 9 February 1824, naval surgeon sailing on Brig Bainbridge for Brazil $2500 life insurance.

Russell, Joseph Lewis: Born in Loudon County, Virginia 7 January 1808/1809. Resides at Harper's Ferry, Virginia. Merchant. 18 January 1837.

Rutter, Thomas B: Born 9 December 1789,Baltimore, Maryland. Resides in Baltimore, Maryland. Cashier of the Farmers & Planters Bank. 29 July 1839.

Baltimore Life Insurance Company Applications

Sabine, Henry: Believed to be Born in Kentucky. Age about 27. Resides in Louisville, Kentucky. Employed as a journeyman Taylor. (Varnum of Louisville, Ky.) Insured by George Hancock. 5 August 1836.

Saltzman, Paul: Born Spangenberg, Kurhess, Germany 26 February 1815. Resides in Baltimore, Maryland at # 11 Poppleton Street. Butcher. 5 October 1848.

Sam, age 21: Born Hanover County, resides in Richmond. 6 January 1834. Application of Mary Thornton of Richmond, Va.

Sam: Born Henrico Co., Va. Age 12. Employed in tobacco Factory. Lives in Richmond, Va. Insured by Thomas W. Doswell, trustee for William P. H. Davenport.

Sam; Age between 17 & 18. Slave belonging to the insurer, William Lyles of Ann Arundel County, Md. Residence near Friendship, Anne Arundel Co. On his master's property. 24 May 1851.

Samuel: Born Hagerstown, Md. Residence Richmond, Va. Slave (cook) to be hired out. Burton Despard, Hanover Co. Va., owner. William Winston Jones, atty.

Sanders, Henry: Born Baltimore, Maryland. Age 25. Resides in Baltimore, Maryland. Butcher. 2 February 1852.

Sandford, James: Born 1 June 1803. Resides in Baltimore, Maryland. 22 September 1838.

Sarah, age 14: Richard F. Danacott, insurer.

Sarah, age 16: Place of birth not given. Residence in Millersville, Anne Arundel County, Md. A slave insured by Mrs. M. E. Woodward of Baltimore, Md.

Schauer, Martin 33: b 12 November 1823 Austria. Residence 108 Chew St. Tailor @ 16 South Street. 11 September 1856.

Schley, William: Born 31 October 1799 in Fredericktown, Frederick Co., Md. 31 August 1831.

Baltimore Life Insurance Company Applications

Schoolar, Thornby E: Born 31 October 1808, Stafford County, Virginia. Resides in Washington, D. C. Clerk in the Washington Arsenal. 24 October 1835.

Schuerman, Charles W: Music Teacher Born 20 November 1818, Westphalia, Germany. Residing in Washington, D. C. 19 January 1853.

Schultz, Cincinnatus: Born 10 March 1828, Baltimore, Maryland. Resides in Baltimore, Maryland. Engaged in the hardware business. Insured by Jefferson Schultz 17 January 1849.

Scott, James: Born 25 August 1800, Hartford, N. Carolina. Resides in Portsmouth, Va. Merchant. 28 November 1836.

Scrivener, John H. Born July 1819, Anne Arundel county, Maryland. Resides in Calvert County, Maryland. Farmer. 16 October 1849.

Seddon, John: Born 9 October 1826, Fredericksburg, Va. Resides in Stafford County, Virginia. Farmer. 9 July 1858.

Seldon, George L: Born Richmond, Virginia, 14 February 1813. U. S. Navy Midshipman, residing in Washington, D. C. 1 January 1835.

Sessford, Jefferson: Born 15 February 1802, Washington, D. C.. Resides in Washington, D. C. Post Office clerk. 9 July 1834.

Sewell, Reuben: Born 30 July 1801, Baltimore, Maryland. Resides in Baltimore, Maryland (Bond Street, Fells Point). Messenger for the Franklin Bank of Baltimore. 15 October 1836. Clerk at the Franklin Bank of Baltimore. 17 April 1838.

Shafer, Abraham Jr: Born 1811, Baltimore County, Maryland. Resides in Baltimore County, farmer. 20 May 1842.

Shaw, Albert: Born Richmond, Va. In 1843. Residence in Richmond. Employed as a house servant. Insured by William Winston Jones 27 March 1857.

Baltimore Life Insurance Company Applications

Shaw, Albert: Born Richmond, Va. In 1843. Resides in Richmond. Employed as a house servant. Insured by William Winston Jones 27 March 1857.

Shaw, Joseph F.: Born in Charles Co., Md. In 1800. Residence near Charlotte Hall, St. Mary's Co., Md. A non practicing physician, engaged in agriculture. 2 September 1851.

Sherburne, John H: Born 4 March 1795, New Hampshire. Resides in Washington, District of Columbia. Clerk in the General Land Office. 28 April 1836.

Sherman, David S: Born in Bridgeport, Connecticut 27 October 1828. Clerk, going to California. 13 January 1849.

Shipley, Sarah Ann: Born 8 April 1793, Baltimore, Maryland. Resides in Baltimore. Housewife. 6 October 1842.

Shoop, Adam: Born Washington Co., Md. 4 June 1807. Residence in Williamsport, Washington Co., Md. Lumber & coal merchant. 15 January 1851.

Shorter, Louisa: B 1835, St. Mary's City, Maryland. House servant (slave?), residing in Baltimore, Maryland. 26 October 853.

Shubrick, William B: Born 31 October 1790. Residence in Baltimore. 26 August 1831.

Silverman, William: Born 7 April 1857. No other data given.

Silvermore, William: Born 13 January 1826, England. Resides in Baltimore, Md. Married. Has three children. Coal & Stone Dealer near Monument St, Baltimore, Md. 7 April 1857.

Silverwood, William: Born in Leister County, England, 13 January 1826. Resides in Baltimore, Maryland. Married, three children. Dealer in coal & stone at Canal Street near Monument. 7 April 1857.

Simmons, Levi: Born in Baltimore, Maryland 20 October 1813. Resides in Baltimore, Maryland. Machinist and engineer.7 August 1850.

Baltimore Life Insurance Company Applications

Simms, John D: Born 29 January 1788, Alexandria, Virginia. Resides in Washington, D. C. Clerk at U. S. Department of the Navy. 29 September 1834.

Simon, 13: Born Hanover, Va. Residence in Richmond, Va. Slave employed in brick making. Insured by William O. Winston for the benefit of Mrs. E. Christian & children, owners.

Simpson, William: Born Aberdeen, Scotland 4 June 1794. Resides in Baltimore, Maryland. Coach maker. 6 February 1837.

Sinn: Born Montgomery Co., Md, 1820. Residence in D. C. on farm of Josiah Brooks. Slave.

Skinner, Thomas: Born 7 May 1803, Elizabeth City County, Virginia. Resides in Richmond, Virginia. Tow Boat operator on the James River. 5 April 1836.

Sloan, John Q.: Born in Baltimore, Maryland . Age 21. Resides in Baltimore, Maryland. Engaged in the mercantile business. 11 March 1850.

Smith, Abraham, Negro. Born 1805 in Baltimore Co. Applicant Nathaniel F. Downing. 11 August 1831.

Smith, Brice: Born in Georgetown, D. C. September 1808. Resides in New York. Attorney. 14 November 1848.

Smith, Gideon: Born Massachusetts 20 July 1793.1 February 1837.

Smith, J. Dean: Born September 1819, Alexandria, Virginia. Resides Baltimore, Maryland. Attorney. Married. 18 July 1860.

Smith, John: Born August 1802, Charles County, Maryland. Formerly resided in Washington, D. C. Now resides in Louisville, Kentucky. Ship's carpenter. 21 December 1836.

Smith, Philip S: Born 16 April 1832, Friendship, Maryland. Merchandiser, residing in Friendship, Maryland. 24 September 1853.

Smith, Rebecca A.: Born 1784, Baltimore, Md. Resides in Baltimore, Md. Housewife. Dennis A. Smith, spouse. 16 May 1833.

Baltimore Life Insurance Company Applications

Smith, Robert M.: Born 20 June 1812 in Baltimore, Md. Residence in Baltimore, Md. Druggist. 21 June 1851.

Smith, Sidney: Born 14 November 1806, Lancaster, Massachusetts. Resides in Mobile, Alabama. Insured by Alabama W. Smith. 20 April 1839.

Smith, W. R: Born in Boston, Massachusetts 2 August 1799. Resides in Fredericksburg, Virginia. Not employed. 2 July 1835.

Smith, William B: Born in Pennsylvania, 25 May 1827. Clerk at the U. S. Treasury Department, Washington, D. C. Resides in Washington, D. C. 31 March 1852.

Smith, William Henry: Born in Virginia 5 November 1822. In the U. S. Navy. 3February 1849.

Smith, William K: B 2 August 1799, Boston, Mass. Resides in Fredericksburg, Va. Miner. Insured by Conrad Hunt of Fredericksburg, Va. I5 July 1848.

Smith, William King: Born 2 August 1799, Boston, Massachusetts. Resides in Fredericksburg, Virginia. 1 July 1835. Insured by John F. Scott 27 March 1845. Gold miner.

Smith, William M.: Born 22 January 1819 in Pundle

Smith, William: Born 6 September 1797, King George Co. Virginia, residence Culpepper Co, Virginia owns stage line & practicing attorney.19 December 1831.

Sommerville, James Jr: Planter, Born 20 February 1811, Prince George's County, Maryland. Resides in Prince George's County, Maryland. 128 December 1852.

Southall, Peyton: Born in Yorktown, Virginia July 1804. Resides in Brooklyn, New York. Courier for the U. S. Government, leaving for Mexico. 8 September 1842.

Spence, Thomas A.: Born in Worcester County, Maryland 21 January 1810. A lawyer, residing in Worcester County, Maryland. 18 October 1848.

Baltimore Life Insurance Company Applications

Spencer, John: Born 27 October 1796, Birmingham, England. Resides in Weavertown, Maryland. Chief of Manufacturing for the Henderson Steel and File Company. 27 February 1852.

Spiller, Edwin N: Salesman, Born in Culpepper, Virginia, residing in Baltimore, Maryland. 4 November 1852.

Staley, George L, 33: Born Sheppardstown, Va. 27 September 1823. Residence Mt. Washington, Baltimore Co., Md. Clergyman & Professor @ Mt. Washington Female College. 31 January 1856.

Stevenson, Harry: Born October 1797 in Baltimore County, Maryland. Resides in Baltimore City. A Lumber merchant. 19 March 1842.

Stewart, L. M.: Born 20 July 1823, Anne Arundel county, Maryland. Resides in Baltimore, Maryland. Grocer. 8 March 1853.

Stewart, Leroy S: B 27 July 1819, Ann Arundel County, Maryland. Resides in Ann Arundel County, Md. Farmer. Possibly relocating to California. 13 February 1852.

Stewart, Mary (colored Girl): resides in Carroll County, Maryland. age not more than 14 years, 20 April 1850. Purchased by Wm. Hogg of Baltimore, Md. 20 April 1850.

Stewart, William H: Born 8 November 1794, Mt. Noly, New Jersey. Resides in Washington, D. C. Furniture Store Owner. 1 February 1838.

Stith, Griffin: Born 1 October 1790, Northampton County, Va. Resides in Baltimore, Md. Merchant. 22 February 1838.

Stocker, James T: Born in Maryland 3 October 1824. Resides in Baltimore, Maryland. Carpenter, going to California.

Stokes, 33: Born Chesterfield Co., Va. Slave, employed at Black Heath Coal Pits. Insured by Theodore Tompkins for William E. Martin.

Baltimore Life Insurance Company Applications

Stover, George: Born 4 May 1789, Portsmouth, New Hampshire. U. S. Navy, captain of the Frigate Constellation in Boston, Mass. Harbor. 25 November 1840.

Streeter, Sebastian: Born 7 July 1810, Weare, New Hampshire. Resides in Baltimore, Maryland. Unemployed editor. 13 June 1839.

Stuart, John Phillip: Born Charles Co., Md. 7 September 1808. farmer, expects to remove to Mississippi in fall.11 September 1839.

Stubbs, Edward: Born November 1785, Dublin, Ireland. Resides in Washington, D. C. Clerk at the U. S. Department of State. 7 September 1832.

Stull, E. W: Note requesting life insurance on self for 3 year period, while in the military service. No other data given. 23 November 1836.

Susan: Born Anne Arundel Co., Md. (near Magothy). Resides in Louisville, Kentucky. House servant insured by Richard N Scott 13 December 1836.

Sutton, Phillip D: Born Anne Arundel co., Md. 18 October 1818. Merchant, age 37. 18 October 1855.

Sweany, Dennis S.: Born 4 April 1802 in Butler County, Pennsylvania. Resides in Baltimore, Maryland. A grocer, living on Caroline Street, going to California.

Sweet, Parker H.: Born in Rhode Island 2 August 1875. Resides in Washington, D. C. A clerk in the land office. 2 March 1848.

Swift, Martha: Slave, residing in Kent County, Maryland. Age about 18. insured by George Pretman, Baltimore, Maryland 20 February 1853.

Sydnor, Fortunaus: Born 29 November 1788 in Norththumberland County, Virginia. Resides in Lynchburg, Virginia. Employed as cashier of the Branch Bank of Virginia. Insured by C. L. Mosby. 29 July 1836.

Sydnor, William: Born Hanover, Va. Age 20. A slave hired to work on the Danville Railroad. Insured by D. Lee Powell. 4 January 1834.

Baltimore Life Insurance Company Applications

Taggart, James B: Born 20 January 1804, Philadelphia, Pennsylvania. Resides in Washington, D. C. Clerk in the General Land Office. 7 April 1837.

Taney, Roger B:, Born Calvert Co. Md. 17 March 1777. **Chief Justice Supreme Court of the United States.** Residence, Baltimore Application also includes certification of death from J. Mason Campbell, executor dated 5 Dec.1864.9 October 1838.

Tanner, William: Born 21 March 1803/04, Kentucky. Resides in Washington, D. C. Postal clerk. 1 May 1839.

Tasistro, L. F: Applicant Charles H. Stewart. Insured is translator in U. S. Dept. of State. Born May 1802 in Dublin, Ireland. 25 October 1851.

Tasistro, L. F.: Translator employed by U. S. Dept. of State, insured by C. M. Pairo.

Tastel, Nicholas: Born Madrid Spain 18 January 1790. Residence Washington, D. C. Clerk U. S. Post Office.5 January 1839.

Tate, Celia: Born Dumfries, Virginia. Age about 34. Resides in Baltimore, Md. Slave for Life. Employed by Luther Ratcliffe. 18 February 1834.

Taylor, Ann Maria: Born in Montgomery County, Maryland 1803. Resides in Washington, D. C. Insured by her spouse Samuel H. Taylor 5 June 1839.

Taylor, Frances (Negro): Born St. Mary's County, Maryland. Resides in Baltimore when not at sea. Seaman, insured by Mary Sloan. 23 December 1835.

Taylor, George H. C.: Resident of California, former resident of Zanesville, Ohio. 27 January 1851.

Taylor, John: Born 28 June 1803, County Down, Ireland. Resides in Washington, D. C. Post Office clerk. 10 February 1835.

Taylor, L. H, 52: Born Md. 14 August 1805. Residence Washington, D. C. Messenger in Trust Dept. 3 December 1856.

Baltimore Life Insurance Company
Applications

Taylor, Samuel H: Born 14 August 1805, Prince
George's County, Maryland. Resides in Washington,
D. C. Watchman at U. S. Department of State. 2
January 1838.
Taylor, William: (Negro): Born St. Mary's County,
Maryland. Resides in Baltimore when not at sea.
Seaman, insured by Mary Sloan. 23 December 1835.
Tella, age 25: Richard F. Danacott
Temple, Ella F: Richmond, Va. 6 February 1834
insures **Jacob,** 26, Born Hanover County, Va.
Employed on the Danville R. R.: **Sorrell, John age
26:** Born Hanover County, Va. employed as driver in
Richmond, Va.
Tenney, Isaac P.: Born in Georgetown, District of
Columbia 20 March 1813. Resides in Georgetown,
D. C. Physician. 18 August 1838.
Terry, Isaiah: Born 12 June 1806. Resides in
Baltimore, Maryland. Millwright. 29 March 1850.
Thayer, Nathaniel H: Born 27 December 1808,
Boston, Massachusetts. Resides at Abington, Harford
county, Maryland. Teacher. 4 November 1840.
Thistle, Hezekiah L. Captain: Born 25 March 1796,
New Hampshire. Resides in Gettysburg,
Pennsylvania. Mechanic. Recently from New
Orleans, La. Inventor of a conveyance for transport
of wounded military & under contract to provide the
same for U. S. Army. Insured by James H. Causter @
Washington, D. C. 31 August 1836.
Thomas, 16: Born King William Co., Va. Residence
Richmond, Va. Employed at Tobacco Factory. Slave
insured by John J. Toler.
Thomas, D. C.: Born 25 May 1821, Norfolk,
Virginia. Resides in Baltimore, Maryland. Merchant.
Married. 19 February 1857.
Thomas, Lucy: a slave: Born Calvert Co., Maryland.
Age 16. Housemaid. Residence in Baltimore,
Maryland.
Thomas, Philip F.: Born September 1810. Resides
in Annapolis, Maryland. Governor of the state of
Maryland. 19 September 1850.

Baltimore Life Insurance Company Applications

Thomas, Warner: Age 54. Born in Virginia. Resides in Baltimore, Md. Employed as a courier. Application date 17 November 1851.

Thomas: Born 12 November 1834, Hanover County, Virginia. Resides in Richmond, Virginia. Slave. 21 November 1851.

Thompson, Emma C. Born: Born 17 March 1800, England. Resides in Georgetown, District of Columbia. Housekeeper. 2 August 1834.

Thompson, John : Born 15 April 1797, Baltimore, Maryland. Resides @ # 70 Henrietta St., Baltimore, Maryland. Carpenter. Insured by Henry Klinefelter 20 November 1837.

Thornton, James Born: Hillsborough County, New Hampshire, 11 July 1800. Resides in Washington, D. C. Second Comptroller of the U. S. Treasury. 27 August 1834.

Thornton, John L: Born August 1780 in Culpepper County, Virginia. Resides in Georgetown, D. C. Gentleman. 5 February 1836.

Tiffany, George Peabody: Born Baltimore, Md. 16 March 1820. Residence in Baltimore. Merchant. 14 February 1857. Beneficiary: Mrs. Ann C. Tiffany.

Tilghman, James: Born 5 February 1793. Resides in Baltimore, Maryland. Employed at the Custom House, Baltimore, Maryland. 24 April 1839.

Timberlake, James: Born 6 November 1816, Fredericksburg, Virginia. Auctioneer, residing in Fredericksburg, Virginia 29 September 1849.

Tom, 22: Born Hanover, Va. Residence in Richmond, Va. Employed as dining room servant. Slave. Insured by Dr. R. T. Coleman.

Tom, 36: Hanover County, Va. Employed on Richmond & Danville RR. 6 January 1834. Benjamin Pollard

Tom: Born in St. Louis, Missouri 1829. Resides in St. Louis, Missouri. House servant (slave), insured by Augustus Gulberth. 10 May 1849.

Baltimore Life Insurance Company Applications

Toney: Slave belonging to Captain William Laughton, Elizabeth City, Virginia. Insured 20 May 1835 by Captain Laughton.

Tonge, Samuel D: Born 18 February 1812, Baltimore, Maryland. Resides in Wheeling, Ohio County, Virginia. Merchant.11 August 1838.

Townsen, Jeremiah: Born 28 January 1818 in Prince George's Co, Md.

Trautman, Gustavus C.: Born 28 October 1824, Germany. Skin dresser, residing in Baltimore, Maryland. 6 February 1852.

Travis: Born in Richmond Co., Va. Age about 54.   Slave, residing i

True, Susanah J.: Born in Fredericksburg, Virginia. Age about 25. Seamstress, residing in Fredericksburg, Virginia. 26 May 1849.

Trustler, William: Born 8 September 1825, Salem township, Muskingum County, Ohio. Farmer, residing in Salem Township, Muskingum County, Ohio. Going to California. 10 April 1850.

Tucker, James: Davenport, England 1706. Blacksmith, Navy Yard Washington D. C. 22 November 1838.

Turner, George W.: Born 20 July 1800, Amherst Co, Virginia. Wife Rebecca Turner.

Turner, Richard James: Born 1 October 1817, Baltimore, Md. Resides in Baltimore, Maryland. Clerk in the Mechanics Bank. 14 February 1842.

Turner, Richard James: Born 27 May 1812, New York. Resides in Louisville, Kentucky. Coal yard superintendent. 18 April 1839.

Twyford, Robert W.: Born 13 March 1818, Accomack County, Virginia. Farmer, residing in Accomack County, Virginia. Harriet Twyford, sister, is named beneficiary. 12 November 1848.

Tyler, Charles: Born in Loudon County, Virginia, March 1778. Resides in Washington, D. C. Clerk in the General Land Office. 20 April 1833.

Baltimore Life Insurance Company
Applications

Tyson, Henry: Born Baltimore, Md. 18 October 1820. Residence in Baltimore Co. Employed at Baltimore & Ohio Railroad as a Master of Machinery. 24 March 1857.

Tyson, Rebecca A: Born in the District of Columbia, 1810. Resides in Louisiana. A. H. Tyson, spouse. 14 February 1848.

U. S. Army Officer, assigned to Green Bay, Wisconsin. 26 November 1838.

Undutch, Nicholas: Born 28 April 1818 in Baltimore, Md. Residence 612 W. Baltimore St., Baltimore, Md. Paperhanger for A. Golder. Mother is Nancy Undutch.

Ungerer, John J.: Born in Switzerland 5 July 1798. Resides in Washington, D. C. Chaplain to the Jefferson Barracks, Missouri. 9 November 1838.

Urana: Age 30. Valued at $700. slave being transported to Savannah, Georgia. Insured by James H. Hammond.

Vallenvilla, Jose: Born in Venezuela. Resides in Baltimore. Traveling to South America. Merchant.

Vanham, William L. Dr: Born 8 December 1807, Bucks County, Pennsylvania. U. S. Naval Doctor. 19 June 1839.

Vanlear, Anna E: Born 28 August 1791, Kent County, Maryland. Resides in Baltimore, Maryland. Housekeeper. 16 January 1841.

VanNess, William J: Born 16 March 1807, Chatham, Columbia County, New York. Resides at #48 Market Place, Baltimore, Maryland. Grocer. 11 January 1839.

VanSant, R. R: Born 28 March 1813. Resides in Baltimore, Maryland. Plans to remove to Mississippi. 8 July 1836.

Vickers, Agnes: Born 1797, London, England. Resides in Baltimore, Maryland. Traveling to London, England. 3 July 1841.

Vincent, Isaac: Born 1806 in Baltimore, Md. Residence in Baltimore, Md. On Johnson St. near Federal Hill. Grain Measurer. 8 June 1846.

Baltimore Life Insurance Company Applications

Vogelman, Charles William: Born in Germany 8 June 1814. Resides in Baltimore. Butcher. 19 November 1835.

Wainwright, R. D. Born in Charlestown, South Carolina, 1781. Resides about 2 miles from Washington, D. C. Commander, U. S. Marine Corp. 24 June 1836.

Walbach, J. J.: Born Fort Constitution, Portsmouth, New Hampshire. Resides at Fort Monroe, Virginia. Lieutenant, U. S. Navy. 14 September 1847.

Walbrook, John J. B: Born in Portsmouth, New Hampshire. Resides in Baltimore, Maryland. Midshipman, U. S. Navy. 17 May 1836.

Walker, Richard J: Born in Fredericksburg, Virgina 19 January 1807. Resides in Fredericksburg, Virginia. Cabinet Maker. 2 April 1836.

Wallbach, J. J. Born: Born 25 April 1811, Portsmouth, New Hampshire. U. S. Naval Officer, residing in Baltimore, Maryland. 31 March 1853.

Wallis, L. Teakle: Born 8 September 1816 in Baltimore, Md. Residence in Baltimore, Md. Lawyer. 11 July 1851.

Ward, James: Born in Calvert County, Maryland. Farmer, residing in Calvert County, Maryland. Age about 42. 16 February 1863.

Ward, James: Farmer Born and residing in Calvert County, Maryland. Born 27 April 1811. 15 December 1852.

Ward, William I.; Born 7 April 1808 in Baltimore, Md. Residence in Baltimore Attorney. 12 February 1851.

Ware, Thomas R.: Born in Fredericksburg, Virginia. Age between 27 & 28. Resides in Fredericksburg, Virginia. U. S. Navy Purser. 19 October 1843.

Ware, William, 37: Born 20 April 1820 Fredericksburg, Va. Residence Fredericksburg, Va., Banker. 8 September, 1856.

Baltimore Life Insurance Company Applications

Warfield, H. W: Born 24 November 1826, Anne Arundel County, Maryland. Resides in Baltimore, Maryland. Annie Warfield, spouse. Traveling to Austrialia by way of England. 21 March 1853.
Warner, Robert, 39: Born Caroline Co., Va. Resides Fredericksburg, Va. Slave. Insured by William White. **Warner, Thomas.** Born in Virginia. Age 54. Residence in Baltimore, Maryland. Employed as a courier. 17 November 1851.
Warner, William: Born 1 July 1826, Connecticut. Bookbinder, residing in Baltimore, Maryland. Daughters, Elizabeth and Virginia are beneficiaries. 15 January 1856. **Washington,** Catherine: Born in Prince George's County, Maryland. Resides in Alexandria, D. C. Chambermaid on steamer. 23 April 1836.
Washington, Joshua (colored man): Born in King George's County, Virginia December 1810. Resides on the mail boat Sydney , plying between Washington & Potomac Creeks. Fireman. 9 January 1836.
Washington, Lund: Born 3 November 1825, Washington, D. C. Resides in Washington, D. C. Student insured by L. D. Quinton 1 December 1837.
Washington, Lund: Born in King George County, Virginia September 1767. Resides in Washington, D. C. Clerk in the office of the Comptroller of the Treasury. 1 June 1833.
Washington, Rachel: Born in Charles County, Maryland. Age about 22. Slave employed as a servant to Mrs. Catherine Ann Pittman, insurer. 1 November 1834.
Waters, Charles R.: Born August 1821, Montgomery county, Maryland. Tobacco inspector, residing in Baltimore, Maryland. 9 April 1853.
Waters, Elizabeth Jane: Born 1787, Dorchester Co., Md. Resides in Baltimore, Md. 8 April 1834.

Baltimore Life Insurance Company Applications

Waters, Ignatius: Born 13 January 1805, Rockville, Maryland. Resides in Clarksburg, Montgomery County, Maryland. Cabinet Maker. 3 November 1841.

Waters, Somerset R.: Born 24 August 1796, Montgomery County, Maryland. Salesman, residing in Baltimore, Maryland. 7 Aparil 1853

Waterworth, Samuel: Born 23 August 1807 in County Down, Ireland. Residence in Baltimore, Md. Weaver. 12 July 1851.

Watkins, T. L. C.: Born 1808. Lieutenant, US. Marines. 1835.

Watson, 24: Born North Carolina. Slave, employed at Black Heath Coal Pits. Insured by Theodore Tompkins for William E. Martin.

Watts, Ebenezer: Born 28 October 1790, Dinwiddie County, Virginia. Resides in Charlottesville, Virginia. Book Seller & Binder, Stationer. 7 March 1837.

Way, David: Cabinet Maker Born (11 June 1818) and residing in Chester, Pennsylvania. Going to California.

Webb, Calvin M: Born 2 March 1807, Bowling Green, Kentucky. Resides in Bowling Green, Kentucky. Clerk in Bank of Kentucky. 23 February 1836.

Webb, Samuel: Born 1821, Massachusetts. Merchant, residing in Baltimore, Maryland. 2 February 1849.

Webster, Daniel: Born in New Hampshire, age about 55. Resides in Boston, Massachusetts. U. S. Senator from Massachusetts. Insured by John Connell, 14 June 1833.

Wedderburn, Alexander: Born in Alexandria, District of Columbia 11 March 1812. Resides in Alexandria, District of Columbia. U. S. Navy Surgeon. 23 October 1838.

Weems, Francis M.: Born 10 December 1810, Virginia. Physician, residing in Tennessee.

Baltimore Life Insurance Company Applications

Weems. Wilson L.: Born 22 November 1810, Anne Arundel County, Maryland Sea Captain, en route to California, insured by Margaret N. Weems4 June 1849.

Weisel, Daniel: Attorney, Born 25 September 1803, Williamsport, Maryland. Resides in Hagerstown, Maryland. 21 August 1852.

Weisiger, W. W: Born 24 December 1803, Chesterfield County, Virginia. Resides in Chesterfield County, Virginia. Farmer. 9 July 1839.

Wellford, Beverly R Jr.,29: Born Fredericksburg, Va. 10 May 1828. Resides Richmond, Va. Attorney. 18 September 1856.

Wellford, J. J. S. 32: Born Fredericksburg, Va. 4 June 1828. Residence Fredericksburg, Va. Physician. 21 June 1856

Wellford, Philip A: Born 24 August 1833, Fredericksburg, Va. Resides sin Fredericksburg, Va. Merchandiser. 9 September 1853.

Wellford, T. P. 29: Born Fredericksburg, Va. 12 September 1828. Residence Fredericksburg, Va. Physician.

Wells, Chase Jr.: Born Chestertown, Rockingham County, New Hampshire. Resides in Baltimore, Md. (Hollins Street). Machine & Can Making. 24 October 1833.

Wentz, Samuel: Born 16 August 1807 in York, Pennsylvania. Resides in Baltimore, Maryland. Book Keeper at the Mechanics Bank of Baltimore. 6 August 1842.

Wentz, William Augustus: Born 5 December 1829, Chambersburg, Pennsylvania. Resides in Baltimore, Maryland. Insured by Samuel A. Wentz 16 January 1849.

Wesley: slave, residing in Calvert County, Maryland. Insured by Benjamin Worrell/ Morrell 20 September 1850.

West, Edward: 17: Born Henrico Co., Va. Age 33. Farmer and salt miller.

Baltimore Life Insurance Company Applications

West, John A: Born in Perry (formerly Cumberland) County, Pennsylvania 12 July 1797. Resides in Louisville, Kentucky. Clerk/Accountant. 20 May 1839.

Wheaton, Sterling Mathias: Born in Raleigh, North Carolina 5 August 1807. Resides in Alabama. Dentist. 12 November 1836.

Wheelwright, George W: Born 19 September 1813, New____, Massachusetts. Resides in Baltimore, Md. Merchant. 26 October 1842.

White, Benet A.: Born 23 December 1803, Hartford, Maryland. Resides in Washington, D. C. Post Office clerk. 14 April 1834.

White, Francis C: Born 1 June 1805, Baltimore, Maryland. Resides at Louisville, Kentucky. Book Keeper. 16 February 1839.

White, Levi S.: Born April 1825, Philadelphia, Pennsylvania. Resides in Baltimore, Maryland. Paperhanger, going to California. 12 January 1849.

White, Mary S: Born 17 March 1822, Baltimore, Md.Resides near Govanstown, Baltimore Co., Md. 7 July 1857.

Whitely, Benjamin: Born Caroline Co., Md. 18 Nov. 1815. Residence in Baltimore. Dry Goods merchant. 20 March 1851.

Whitely, Samuel: Born 18 March 1820, Wakefield, York County, England. Iron molder, residing in Fredericksburg, Virginia. . 5 April 1854.

Whitely, William S.: Born 18 April 1826 in Caroline Co., Md. Residence in Baltimore, Md, Merchant. 17 October 1851.

Whiting, George C: Born 29 December 1816, Loudon County, Virginia. Resides in Washington, D. C. Clerk in the General Land Office. 2 April 1838.

Whiting, Joseph P.: Born in Maryland 9 March 1800. 14 March 1849.

Whittaker, Nathaniel B: Born November 1797, Havre de Grace, Maryland. Resides in Baltimore, Maryland. Dry Goods Store operator. 17 March 1832.

Baltimore Life Insurance Company Applications

Whyte, William Pinkney: Born in Baltimore, Maryland 9 August 1824. Lawyer, residing in Baltimore, Maryland at #103 St. Paul Street. 1 November 1849.

Wickes, Charles H.: Born in Chestertown, Maryland, July 1820. Lawyer, residing in Chestertown, Maryland. 16 March 1849.

Wierman, Charles: Born 15 October 1877, Pennsylvania. Clerk, residing in Washington, D. C. Insured by Nathan Sargent. 2 November 1809.

Wiggins, Daniel A.: Born 14 March 1784, Long Island, New York. Resides at Annapolis, Maryland. 26 September 1838.

Wilcox, Charles G.: Born Philadelphia, Pa. 25 November 1877. Residence in Washington, D. C. Office Clerk. 22 March 1851.

Wilcox, Charles: Born in Pennsylvania. Age about 43 –45. Resides at Washington, D. C. Office Clerk. Insured by Darius Clagett 19 October 1838.

William, 12: Residence in Richmond, Va. Employed in Tobacco Factory. Slave. Insured by John Darracott.

William, 15: Born King William Co., Va. Residence Richmond, Va. Employed at Tobacco Factory. Slave insured by John J. Toler.

William, 40: Born Richmond, Va. Residence in Richmond, Va. Cook. Insured by William Winston Jones 16 September 1854.

William, age 10: 6 April 1834. Richmond, Va. Born in Upper, Va. Works in tobacco factory. Thomas Pollard, applicant,

William: Slave, age about 30 Born in Washington, D. C. Resides in Georgetown, D. C. insured by Henry Addison.

Williams, Benjamin: Born 17 September 1784, Virginia. Warden, D. C. Penitentiary. 9 December 1831.

Williams, Charles A: Born 4 July 1804m Palmyra, N. Y. Resides in Washington, D. C. Postal clerk. 18 May 1835.

Baltimore Life Insurance Company Applications

Williams, Felix R: Born in Baltimore, Maryland 30 May 1807. Resides at 78 W. Pratt Street, Baltimore, Maryland. Practitioner of Medicine. 2 March 1842.

Williams, George T: Born 1791, Goochland County, Virginia. Resides in Lynchburg, Virginia. Manufacturer & dealer in tobacco. 15 March 1845. (2nd application 1 January 1838 gives 21 February 1792 as birth date).

Williams, Hampton C: Born 10 July 1807, Clark County, Georgia. Resides at Georgetown, D. C. Auditor's Office clerk.1 April 1835.

Williams, James: Born in Maryland 1795. Resides in Norfolk, Virginia. Lieutenant, U. S. Navy. 27 October 1835.

Williams, John: Born 14 October 1809, Harford County, Maryland. Clerk, residing in Baltimore, Maryland. 5 July 1849.

Williams, Priscilla, 26: Born St. Mary's Co., Md. Residence on Mr. Hartman's Farm, Sulphur Springs, Baltimore Co., Md. Slave. Benefits payable to Rebecca Sommerville. 2 August 1856.

Williams, Priscilla: 26: Born St. Mary's Co., Md. Resides on Mr. Hartman's Farm, Sulphur Springs, Baltimore Co., Md. Slave, benefits payable to Rebecca Sommerville. 2 August 1856.

Williams, William 39: Born Norfolk, Va. Residence Baltimore, married, porter in Dry Goods Store. Slave insured by Pegram, Paynter & Davis. 21 August 1856.

Williams, William P. 30: Born Virginia 14 November 1826. Residence Spotsylvania Co, Va. Farmer. 19 August 1856.

Williams, William, 39: Born Norfolk, Va. Resides Baltimore, married, porter in Dry Goods Store. Slave insured by Pegram, Paynter & Davis. 21 August 1856.

Willingham, Charles: Born 1807, resides in Baltimore, Maryland. Coachman for Jerome N. Bonaparte. (son of Betsy Bonaparte.), insurer. 25 November 1834.

Baltimore Life Insurance Company Applications

Willis, Benjamin F.: Born 13 November 1819, King & Queen County, Virginia. Clerk, residing in Baltimore, Maryland. 2 July 1849.

Wilson, 19: Born Hanover Co., Va. Residence Henrico Co., Va. Farm laborer. Slave insured by William P. Darracott 15 December 1856.

Wilson, David: Born February 1798. Resides in Washington, D. C. Chief of U. S. Capital Police. 1 July 1835.

Wilson, George: Born in the District of Columbia. Age about 27. Steamboat employee, residing in Georgetown, District of Columbia, insured by Samuel Baker 6 April 1853..

Wilson, James C: Born 5 May 1791, Alexandria, District of Columbia. Resides in Georgetown, District of Columbia. Clerk. 28 June 1833.

Wilson, John Kilty: Born 26 January 1823, Baltimore, Maryland. Midshipman, U. S. Navy, residing in Baltimore, Maryland 16 February 1853.

Wilson, John M: Born in Fredericksburg, Va. July 1813. Resides in Richmond, Va. Merchant. 15 November 1836.

Wilson, Richard: Born 4 February 1852, London, England. General agent residing in Baltimore, Maryland. 4 February 1852.

Wilson, Robert: Born 22 October 1811, County Cairn, Ireland. Resides in St. Louis, Missouri. Going to California. 26 March 1849.

Wilson, William T.: Born 14 March 1797, Calvert County, Maryland. Farmer and minister, residing in Calvert County, Maryland. 8 December 1849.

Winder, Mary: Born 24 May 1850, Baltimore county, Maryland. Resides in Baltimore, Maryland in the home of John Philpot. 5 July 1850.

Winder, William H: Born 12 February 1808, Baltimore, Md. residence Baltimore but expects to remove to Philadelphia, Pa.31 January 1832

Wing, John: Born 21 March 1816, Maine. Resides in Lockhaven, Pa. Lumberman. 16 January 1852.

Baltimore Life Insurance Company Applications

Winslow, Robert : Born 1 January 1830, Philadelphia, Pennsylvania. Resides in Baltimore, Maryland. Type caster. 7 January 1853.

Winston, Wm. C: Hanover County, Va. 6 February 1834 insures **Edmund**, Born 1829, Hanover County, Va. Employed on Va. & Tenn. R.R. **Richard**, Born Sept 1826; **Frank**, April 1828; **London**, August 1828. National Loan Fund Life Assurance Co. of London formerly insured all.

Wolf, John P.: Born 18 July 1814 in Pennsylvania. Clerk. Resides in Washington D. C. 8 November 1855.

Wolf, John R.: Born in Pennsylvania, 18 July 1814. Resides in Washington, D. C. Clerk. 28 July 1849.

Wolf. John P: Born 18 July 1814 in Pennsylvania. Clerk. Residence in Washington D. C. 8 November 1855.

Wolford, Henry: Born 4 May 1806, Philadelphia, Pennsylvania. Resides in Louisville, Kentucky. Coal trader. 6 July 1839.

Wood, James M: Born 2 May 1833 in Prince George's Co., Md. Carpenter. Insured by Samuel Jones of Anne Arundel Co., Md. 13 December 1855.

Woodberry, Joseph: Born in Maine 25 January 1804. Resides in Portland, Maine. Master of the brig ' Harriet'. 1 June 1836.

Woodside, James D.: Born 12 October 1790, Philadelphia, Pa. Resides in Washington., D. C. Clerk at the office of the Register of the U. S. Treasury. 30 April 1838.

Woodward, Henry: Born 30 July 1803, Anne Arundel County, Maryland. Resides at Florence, Stewart's County, Georgia. Merchandiser. 31 October 1838.

Worthington, Brice T.: Born 2 April 1820 in Anne Arundel Co., Md. Residence in Annapolis, Md. Attorney at Law. 28 July 1851.

Baltimore Life Insurance Company Applications

Worthington, George Y.: Born 11 July 1819, Baltimore, Maryland. Resides in Hockley, Howard County, Maryland. Merchant. Spouse, Elizabeth T. Worthington. 12 April 1850.

Worthington, Nicholas I: Born 10 April 1817, Anne Arundel Co., Md. Farmer & County Sheriff, residing in Anne Arundel County, Md.

Wright, Benjamin C: Born 7 December 1808, Berkley County, Virginia. Resides in Baltimore, Maryland. A retailer of dry goods. 4 February 1842.

Wyatt, Silas: Born in King & Queen county, Virginia 1 January 1807. Resides in Richmond, Virginia. Wholesale and retail grocer. 13 August 1836.

Wysham, Joseph: Born Baltimore, Md. 26 January 1832. Resides in Baltimore, single, unemployed. 4 October 1855

Young, Alexander: Born Baltimore, Md. 5 September 1806. Residence in Baltimore. Employed as clerk at customhouse. 21 March 1857.

Young, Josias: Born in Prince George's County, Maryland. Age about 65. Farmer, residing in Price George's County, Maryland. Insured by Edward Reynolds 13 August 1850.

Young, Nicholas: Born 27 September 1808, Martinsburg, Virginia. Resides in Lancaster, Fairfield County, Ohio. Saddler. 6 November 1837.

Baltimore Life Insurance Company Applications

A

Abbett, Thomas M., 1
Abbot, Thomas M., 16
Adams, George, 1
Adams, Isaac;
  Thomas, 1
Addison, Henry, 91
Addison, John C., *1*
Addison, John, 1
Alexander Claxton, 16
Alfred, Joseph, 2
Allen, A. W., 85
Allen, James W., 2
Allen, Thomas, 2
Allison, Henry, 2
Anderson, George W, 2
Anderson, Richard, 2
Armour, James, 3
Arthur, Robert, 3
Atkinson, Joseph M. Rev., 3
Austen, James H, 3
Austin, Henry, 3

B

Baden, John R, 4
Bagby, Arthur P., 44
Bailey, Thomas T., 4
Baker, Samuel, 93
Baldwin, Daniel, 4
Baldwin, David, 4
Baldwin, Frederick, 4
Ball, John L., 4
Bankhead, Theophilis, 4
Banks, George, 4
Barbour, Andrew, 4
Barnes, Abraham, 4
Barnes, Frances Ida, 5
Barnes, J. T. Mason, 5
Barney, John, 5
Barnum, Augustus, 5
Barton, Thomas, 5
Barry, William R., 5
Basley, Benjamin, 5
Bass, Colin, 6
Battee, Dennis H, 6
Baurman, Ignatius, 50
Baxter, Sydney S, 6
Beach, Miles, 6
Beall, Benjamin, 6
Beam, Robert M, 6
Beardsley, Charles, 25
Beers, Isaac, 6
Bell, George B, 6
Bell, John W, 6
Bell, Thomas, 20
Belt, Thomas H, 6
Bennett, Henry, 6
Bentz, Samuel, 6
Bernard, E. F., 4
Bernard, Overton, 7
Berryman, A. H, 7
Betts, Royston, 7
Bibb, George W, 7

Baltimore Life Insurance Company Applications

Baltimore Life Insurance Company Applications

Brown, George W, 11

Brown, Harriet, 11

Brown, J. W., 11

Bryan, Joseph, 11

Buchanan, Franklin, 11

Buchinal, James, 11

Buddy, John, 12

Bullock, Erasmus, 12

Burchard, Matthew H, 12

Burchard, Matthew H., 12

Burke, James M, 12

Burns, Francis, 2

Bustun, John Born, 12

   David, 27

   H. W., 71

   Lote, 70

C

Cain, Gustavius, 12

Camp, John G., 12

Campbell, Bernard U. /W, 12

Carey, John L, 12

Cargill, Elbert, 12

Carmichael, Edward H., 13

Carmichael, James, 13

Carnes, Stephen D., 20

Carothers, Andrew, 13

Carothers, Andrew, 13

Carpenter, William H., 13

Carr, Dabney L., 13

Carr, Overton; William, 13

Carrington, Louisa, 28

Carson, Joshua, 14

Carter, George, 14

Carter, Robert W., 84

Carter, Robert; Elizabeth O., 14

Causter, James H., 82

Chalmers, Charles, 14

Chambers, John J., 14

Chappell, Philip L., 14

Chew, Henry M, 15

Chew, John James, 13, 15

Chew, Thomas I (J ?), 15

Claggett, Darius, 91

Clare, Thomas, 15

Clark, James, 15

Clark, Shelby, 16

Clarke, Merriwether Lewis, 16

Clarke, Robert P., 16

Clarke, W. B., 16

Claybrook, George, 16

Claybrooke, George, 16

Clemens, Augustus D, 16

Baltimore Life Insurance Company Applications

Baltimore Life Insurance Company Applications

Baltimore Life Insurance Company Applications

Flusser, Charles T., 28
Foley, James S., 28
Foose, Edward A., 28
Ford, Stephen C., 28
Foreman, Moses, 28
Forest, Mary L., 28
Forrest, Samuel, 28
Forry, Samuel Dr., 28
Fowler, James Martin, 28
Fowler, John H., 13
France, Lewis H., 29
Francicus, John, 29
Freeland, Egbert, 29
French, Elizabeth, 29
Frink Harvey, 29
Funk, Solomon, 29
Fustug (Fustieg?)J., 29

G

Gales, James, 29
Gallagher, James, 30
Gallegher, John, 28
Gansvoort, Hun, 30
Gardner, F., 55
Gardner, William H., 30
Garland, Edward, 30
Garland, Hudson M. Jr, 30
Gaskins, James R., 30
Gaskins, John W., 30

Gatchel, William H, 30
Geganbach, John, 30
Gell, George M., 31
George, Robert, 31
Gibson, Alexander, 31
Giles, Aquila P., 31
Giles, John, 31
Gilman, Charles Hamilton, 32
Gilpin, Charles, 32
Ginn, Peter D., 65
Gittings, John, 32
Gittings, Lambert, 32
Glynn, Anthony G., 32
Godey, Walter, 32
Goings/Goines, Richard E., 32
Goode, George, 32
Goodwin, Arthur, 32
Goodwin, Charles, 32
Goodwin, Lyde, 32
Gordon, Alexander George, 32
Gorsuch, William, 1
Gouge, William M., 67
Gough, Patrick, 33
Gould, James F.
Gould, James, 33
Gould, James, 33Gwynn, John R, 34
Graff, Frederick, 33
Graham, Thomas J., 33

Baltimore Life Insurance Company Applications

Gray, Jane, 33
Green, Joshua, 33
Griffith, Romulus
    R., 33
Grigsby, Francis
    Frost
Grover, Charles, 34
Grubb, Sam, 34
Gulberth, Augustus,
    83
Gwathney, Samuel,
    34
Gwynn, William, 34
    Henry N., 34
    Jane, 33

H

Haarmon, John;
    Ellen P.; Mary
    Louisa;, 36
Hagner, Alexander
    B, 34
Hagner, John R., 34
Haines, Charles, 34
Hale, Phillip, 48
Hale, Phillip;, 34
Hale, William H, 35
Hall, Caroline;
    Francis C.;
    Richard W., 35
Hall, Joseph, 35
Hammond, James
    H., 85
Hammond, Richard
    P, 35
Hampton, Robert B,
    35
Hancock, George, 74
Hands, Washington,
    35

Handy, John H., 35
Handy, John jr., 36
Handy, William, 36
Hanna, William, 36
Hanson, Isaac K., 36
Hardesty, C. R, 36
Hardie, Robert, 36
Hardy, Robert, 36
Hardy, Thomas Dr.,
    36
Harper, Francis, 36
Harris, Carey A., 37
Harris, Edgar, 37
Harrison, Alexander,
    37
Harrison, Gustavius,
    37
Harrison, Horace N.,
    37
Harrison, Samuel S,
    37
Harrison, William
    H., 37
Hart, W., 38
Hawkins, H. L., 38
Haywood, Thomas,
    38
Heald, John R., 38
Heiner, John, 38
Hepburn, John W.,
    39
Herndon, Brodie S,
    39
Herring, Henry, 39
Hickman, N, 39
Hickman, N., 39
Higgins, Edward, 39
Hilberg, Frederick,
    39
Hilliary, L., 37

Baltimore Life Insurance Company
Applications

Baltimore Life Insurance Company Applications

Johnson, Reverdy, 45

Johnston, Fayette, 46

Johnston, Francis, 46

Johnston, Gabriel, 46

Johnston, Robert N, 46

Johnston, Virginia Elizabeth, 46

Jones, George W, 46

Jones, Walter F., 46

Jordan, William M., 46

Joyce, Henry & John, 47

K

Kahissowski, Henry K., 47

Kane, Rufus K., 47

Katz, Marcus, 47

Keeling, David F., 47

Keller, Charles M., 47

Kellog, John H., 47

Kellum, Edward M., 47

Kennard, Alexander A., 47

Kerr, John Bozman, 47

Keyworth, Robert, 48

King, J. D., 48

King, James D., 48

Kitzmiller, Archibald M., 48

Klockeither, Lewis, 48

Knight, John L., 27

Kortwright, Cornelius H., 48

Krager, Henry, 48

Krebs, Charles W., 48

Krudenis, Paul Baron, 48

Kurtz, J. D, 48

Kurtz, J. D., 48

L

Lackland, M. C., 48

Lafitte, Henry, 48

Landis, Joseph A., 49

Larned, Charles H., 49

Latrobe, John H., 49

Lattimans, Alexander Frederick, 49

Laughton, William Captain, 84

Laurence, Col. A. N, 49

Laurensen, James, 49

Lawson, Henry,jr; Nancy Jane; Mary Ann, 49

Lea, Albert Miller, 50

Leary, Cornelius. L. L, 50

Leary, Thomas H. H., 50

Lee, Catherine, 50

Baltimore Life Insurance Company Applications

Leftwich, Augustine, 9

Lehmanousky, Edward, 50

Lendrum, Thomas W, 50

Leonnard, William T. Dr., 50

Levin, L. C., 50

Levin, Lewis C, 50

Lewis, Edward W., 51

Lewis, John T., 51

Lightner, James, 51

Lindsey, G. F., 51

Linville, Maria, 51

Little, Andrew M., 51

Little, Charles, 51

Livingston, James, 51

Long, Cornelius, 52

Long, Ellis B., 52

Loughery, A., 52

Love, R. H., 35

Lowery, James H., 52

Loyall, William, 52

Lucas, Charles, 52

Lucas, Ellen, 52

Luce, John B., 52

Ludwig, Samuel, 52

Lusborough, Harriet, 53

Lussborough, Harriet, 53

Lyles, Barbara Ann, 53

Lyles, William, 74

Lyman, William O, 53

Lynde, Richard D., 53

Vernon J., 23

M

Mackale, Richard G., 53

Maddox, John H., 53

Magahey, James O., 53

Magruder, John B., 53

Marr, james, 54

Marshall, John Alexander, 54

Marston, William A., 44

Martin, Anderson, 54

Masi, Serapheim, 54

Mason, J. Thompson, 54

Mason, William, 54

Mathews, William Jesse, 55

Matlock, Richard, 55

Maulsby, William P., 55

Maxey, Virgil, 55

Maxey/Maxcy, Virgil, 55

Mayer, Charles F., 59

Mayer, Charles F: of Lewis, 55

McAllister, Robert, 55

Baltimore Life Insurance Company Applications

McClellan, David W. B, 55
McClellan, William, 55
McColm, Edward M., 55
McConnell, Edward, 56
McCormick, James, 56
McCullough, William, 56, 77
McDonald, Grace, 56
McDonald, Michael, 56
McGee, J. W, 56
McGehee, Lewis, 56
McGinnis, Francis I, 56
McGuire, Hugh H., 56
McIntosh, James, 56
McKean, H. Pratt, 56
McKee, John, 57
McKeever, Issac, 57
McKenney, John., 27
McKenney, William, 57
McLane, Allen, 57
McLaughlin, Augustus, 57
McLaughlin, William, 57
McLean, Cornelius, 57
McNeal, William, 3

McNeir, George Jr, 57
McPherson, John, 57
Meade, Holmes, 57
Medcalfe, Charles, 58
Meeds, John Davis, 58
Mele, Francis, 58
Mercer, William F., 58
Meriwether, William, 58
Merker, Andreew, 58
Merriken, James, 58
Merryman, Samuel, 58
Micows, William, 58
Middleton, Reuben, 58
Middleton, William G., 58
Milhausen, Henry, 58
Miller, Edwin A., 59
Miller, William H., 51
Mills, Enoch G., 59
Minifie, William, 59
Mitchell, Alexander, 59
Mitchell, Elizabeth, 59
Montell, Francis, 59
Montgomery, Alexander, 59
Montgomery, Robert G., 59

Baltimore Life Insurance Company Applications

Moody, Theodore, 60

Moore, Alfred L., 60

Moore, P. T, 60

Moore, Thomas J., 60

Mordical, Sam, 60

Morell, William H., 60

Morfit, Robert, 42

Morgan, C. C., 60

Morrell, Benjamin, 43, 89

Morrell, Joshua, 60

Morrison, Samuel A., 60

Morson, Arthur A., 60

Mosby, C. L., 80

Mosby, Edward C., 61

Mosby, William W., 61

Moulton, Ferdinand, 61

Mulhausen, Henrich B, 61

Mulhausen, Henrich B., 61

Muller, August, 61

Murphy, Thomas S., 61

Murray, James, 61

Murray, John, 61

Murray, Samuel, 62

Muse, William T, 62

N

Neal, Joseph, 62

Nearman, Charles, 62

Newell, Lloyd R., 62

Nicholson, August A., 62

Nollner, Jacob, 62

Norris, John Lauren, 62

Nutwell, John L., 63

O

Oden, George, 63

Odersley, Harriet, 63

Ogden, William L., 63

Ogle, Atkin S., 63

Osbourne, Charles F., 63

Ould, Robert, 63

Owen, John, 63

P

Pairo, C. M., 81

Pairo, Charles W., 63

Palmer, Harriet, 63

Palmer, Harriet, 63

Palmer, Thomas

Parish, John G., 64

Parker, Foxhall A., 64

Parker, Mrs. Ellen E, 64

Pattterson, Carlisle S., 64

Payne, William W., 64

Peabody, Adolphus W., 64

Baltimore Life Insurance Company Applications

Pebbles, C. G., 64
Peebles, C. G., 65
Pendleton, John S., 64
Peterkin, Joshua, 65
Peters, Jesse T, 65
Pettrich, Ferdinand, 65
Phenix, Thomas, 65
Pinkney, Henry, 66
Piper, James, 66
Pittman, Catherine Ann, 87
Plant, James K., 66
Pleasant, C. M., 25
Pleasants, Charles E. Rev., 66
Plitt, Charles, 66
Plympton, William, 66
Poe, Nelson, 66
Poindexter, T. B, 66
Pollard, Camilla M., 9
Porter, Henry, 66
Posey, Benjamin, 67
Potter, Zabdiel, 67
Powell, D. Lee, 80
Prather, Henrietta M., 67
Prentiss, William, 67
Preston, Robert J., 67
Prevost, Lewis M., 67
Price, A. M., 67
Price, John, 67
Price, Thomas, 67
Prout, Sarah E., 67

Q

Quissonberry, William, 67

R

Ragsdale, Anna Maria McLean, 68
Ragsdale, Susan Eliza, 68
Raisin, Horace, 68
Ramsey, Charles R., 68
Ramsey, William, 68
Ramsey, Wordsworth, 68
Randolph, G. W., 68
Ratcliffe, Luther, 81
Redd, John, 68
Reeder, William A., 68
Reeder, William, 58
Reese, John E., 68
Reich, Phillip, 69
Reinhardt, Henry, 69
Retan, Samuel, 69
Reynolds, Edward, 45, 62
Rice, Francis A., 69
Richards, Adolph, 69
Richardson, Edward D, 70
Richardson, George R.; George, 70
Ricords, John Robert, 69
Riddle, Robert, 70
Ridgeaway, William, 70

Baltimore Life Insurance Company Applications

Ridgely, James;
  James P.; Charles
  L.;, 70
Ridgely, Mary
Ridgely, Richard H.
  L., 71
Riley, John, 71
Ringgold,
  Cadusladu, 71
Ritchie, William B.,
  71
Rittenhouse, F., 71
Rittenhouse, John B,
  71
Roane, William, 71
Robbins, Julius A.
Roberts, Christiana
  G, 72
Roberts, Christiana
  G., 72
Robertson, John T;
  Maria M., 72
Robinson William
  Jr, 72
Robinson, John, 72
Rodewald, Henry,
  72
Rogers, Gilbert Jr.,
  72
Rooker, Jabez Berry,
  72
Rosenstock, George,
  17
Rosenthal, Augusta
  Sophia, 73
Ross, John, 73
Ross, N., 67
Ross, Richard H., 73
Ross, Robert T, 73

Rothreck, Larkin J.,
  73
Rowe, Dexter, 73
Royall, John J., 9
Royall, John M, 73
Ruckle, John, 73
Russell, Joseph
  Lewis, 73
Rutter, Thomas B.,
  73

S

Sabine, Henry, 74
Saltzman, Paul, 74
Sanders, Henry, 74
Sandford, James, 74
Schley, William, 74
Schoolar, Thornby
  E., 75
Schuerman, Charles
  W, 75
Schuerman, Charles
  W., 75
Schultz, Cincinnatus,
  75
Scott, James, 75
Scott, Richard N., 80
Scrivener, John H.,
  75
Seddon, John, 75
Seldon, George L.,
  75
Sessford, Jefferson,
  75
Sewell, Reuben, 75
Shaw, Albert, 76
Shaw, Joseph F, 76
Sherburne, John H.,
  76

Baltimore Life Insurance Company Applications

Sherman, David, 76
Shipley, Sarah H., 76
Shoop, Adam, 76
Shorter, Louisa, 76
Shubrick, William B, 76
Silverman, William, 76
Silvermore, William, 76
Silverwood, William, 76
Simmons, Levi, 76
Simms, John D., 77
Simpson, William, 77
Skinner, Thomas, 77
Sloan, John Q., 77
Smith, Abraham, Negro, 77
Smith, Brice., 77
Smith, Dennis A.; Rebecca A.; John, 77
Smith, Gideon, 77
Smith, J. Dean, 77
Smith, John M., 8
Smith, Philip S., 77
Smith, Robert M, 78
Smith, W. R., 78
Smith, William B., 78
Smith, william Henry, 78
Smith, William K., 78
Smith, William King, 78
Smith, William, 78

Sommerville, James jr, 78
Sommerville, James jr., 78
Spence, Thomas A., 78
Spencer, John, 79
Spiller, Edwin N, 79
Stevenson, Ferdinand M., 25
Stevenson, Harry, 79
Stewart, L. M., 79
Stewart, Leroy S., 79
Stith, Griffin, 79
Stocker, James T., 79
Stover, George, 80
Streeter, Sebastian, 80
Stuart, John Phillip, 80
Stull, E. W., 80
Sullivan, P. Henry, 35
Summerville, W., 65
Sutton, Phillip D, 80
Sweany, Dennis S., 80
Sweet, Parker H., 80
Swift, Martha, 80
Sydnor, Fortunatus, 80
Sydnor, William, 80

T

Taggert, James B., 81
Taney Roger, 81
Tasistro, L. F., 81
Tastel, Nicholas, 81

Baltimore Life Insurance Company Applications

Tate, Celia, 81
Taylor, Ann Maria;
  Frances, 81
Taylor, George H.
  C., 81
Taylor, Samuel H.,
  82
Tenney, Isaac, 82
Terry, Isaiah, 82
Thayer, Nathaniel
  H., 82
Thistle, Hezekiah L.
  Captain, 82
Thomas, D. C., 82
Thomas, Philip F.,
  82
Thompson, John, 83
Thornton, James, 83
Tilghman, James, 83
Timberlake, James,
  83
Tonge, Samuel D, 84
Trautman, Gustavas
  C., 84
True, Susannah J.,
  84
Trustler, William, 84
Tucker, James, 84
Turner, George W,
  84
Turner, Richard
  James, 84
Twyford, Robert W.,
  84
Tyler, Charles, 84
Tyson, Rebecca, 85

U

Undutch, Nicholas;
  Nancy, 85

Ungerer, John J, 85

V

Vallenvilla, Jose, 85
Vance, Samuel, 57
Vanham, William L.
  Dr, 85
Vanlear, Anna E, 85
VanNess, William J,
  85
VanSant, R. R, 85
Vickers, Agnes, 85
Vincent, Isaac, 85
Vogelman, Charles
  William, 86

W

Wainwright, R. D,
  86
Walbach, J.J. 86
Walbrook, John J. B,
  86
Walker, Richard J,
  86
Wallis, L. Teakle, 86
Ward, James, 86
Ward, William I., 86
Ware, Thomas R.,
  86
Warfield, H. W, 87
Warner, Robert, 87
Warner, William, 87
Washington, Rachel,
  87
Waters, Charles R;
  Elizabeth Jane, 87
Waters, Somerset R,
  88

Baltimore Life Insurance Company Applications

Waterworth, Samuel, 88

Watts, Ebenezer, 88

Way, David, 88

Webb, Calvin M; Christopher C., 88

Webster, Daniel, 88

Wedderburn, Alexander, 88

Weems, Francis M., 88

Weems, Wilson L., 89

Weisel, Daniel, 89

Weisiger, W. W, 89

Wellford, Beverly R Jr, 89

Wellford, Philip A., 89

Wells, Case Jr., 89

Wells, T. L. C., 88

Wentz, Samuel, 89

Wentz, William Augustus, 89

West, John A, 90

Wheaton, Sterling Mathias, 90

Wheelwright, George W, 90

White, Benet A.; Francis C, 90

White, Levi S., 90

White, Mary S, 90

White, William, 87

Whitely, Benjamin, 90

Whitely, Samuel, 90

Whitely, William S, 90

Whiting, George C, 90

Whiting, Joseph P., 90

Whitlock, George, 21, 39

Whittaker, Nathaniel B, 90

Whyte, William Pinkney, 91

Wickes, Charles H., 91

Wickham, Henry, 25

Wierman, Charles, 91

Wiggins, Daniel A, 91

Wilcox, Charles G., 91

Wilcox, Charles, 91

Willford, Charles C., 13

Williams, Benjamin, 91

Williams, Charles A, 91

Williams, Felix R, 92

Williams, George T, 92

Williams, Hampton C, 92

Williams, James, 92

Williams, John, 92

Williams, Priscilla, 92

Willingham, Charles, 92

Willis, Benjamin F., 93

Baltimore Life Insurance Company Applications

Wilson, David, 93
Wilson, George, 93
Wilson, John Kilty
Wilson, Richard, 93
Wilson, Robert, 93
Wilson, William T.,
　93
Winder, Mary, 93
Winder, William H,
　93
Wing, John, 93
Winslow, Robert, 94
Wolf, John R., 94
Wolf. John P, 94
Wolford, Henry, 94
Wood, James M, 94
Woodberry, Joseph,
　94
Woodside, James D,
　94
Woodward, Henry,
　94

Woodward, M. E.,
　74
Worrell, Benjamin,
　43, 89
Worthington, Brice
　T, 94
Worthington,
　George W., 45
Worthington,
　George Y., 95
Worthington,
　Nicholas I, 95
Wright, Benjamin C,
　95
Wyatt, Silas, 95

Y

Young, Alexander,
　95
Young, Josias, 7
Young, Josias, 95

Appendix One

**An Act to incorporate the Baltimore Life
Insurance Company.**

Section 1. Be it enacted by the General
Assembly of Maryland, That John Gibson,
Edward G. Woodyear, John J. Donaldson,
Robert Oliver, W. W. Taylor, S. J. Donaldson, Joseph Todhunter, Alexander 'Donald.
Henry Didier, Thomas L. Emory, Alexander
Fridge, Edward Didier, and Benjamin D.
Higdon, and such other persons as
may become associated with them for that
purpose, are hereby created a body politic and
corporate, by the name and style of The
Baltimore Life Insurance Company, and
by that name and style shall be capable of suing
and being sued, in any court of law or equity, of
purchasing, holding, improving and conveying,
any estate, real, personal or
mixed; to make, have and use, a common seal,
and the same to change or renew at pleasure;
and generally to do every other act or thing
necessary to carry into effect this act, or to
promote the object and design of this
corporation.

Sec. 2- And be it enacted, That the capital stock
of this corporation shall be fifty thousand
dollars, to be divided

into one thousand shares of fifty dollars each,
and the same shall be paid in manner following:
Two dollars in five days after the election of
directors as hereinafter provided for, and the
remainder in six equal payments in four, eight,
twelve, sixteen, twenty and twenty-four months
thereafter,
notes with surety being given by each
stockholder for the

payments aforesaid; which said capital stock
may be increased from time to time, at the
discretion of president and directors, to three
hundred thousand dollars, by additional
subscriptions, in such manner as they may think
proper; and if any stockholder shall refuse or
neglect to make
the payments aforesaid, he or she shall cease to
be a stockholder of said corporation, and his or
her share or shares
may, at the discretion of the president and
directors, be

forfeited, and the same may be sold by said
corporation in any manner it may think proper;
Provided however, that said stockholders shall
not be released from his or her liability on
account of any loss or any risk taken before said
forfeiture, but said corporation may sue him or
her for his
or her proportion of said loss, not. exceeding
that part of his or her original subscription
which he or she shall have
so refused or neglected to pay.

Sec. 3. And be it enacted, That there shall be a meeting of the stockholders on the first Monday in April next, at such place and time as the three first persons named in
this act shall appoint, ten days notice being first given, and on the same day in every year thereafter, for the election of eight directors from the stockholders, each share
being entitled to one vote, and a plurality of votes being sufficient for an election; which directors shall, within ten days thereafter, choose a president who shall also be a stockholder; any five directors, or four with the president, shall constitute a quorum; and if it should so happen that the said stockholders shall omit to make an election of directors on the first Monday of April in any year during the continuance of this act, then and in such case, it shall be lawful for the stockholders to make said electron on
some other day to be appointed by the president and directors for the time being, ten days notice being given in some
newspaper printed in the city of Baltimore of the time and place of holding said election; and in case of death, resignation, disqualification by ceasing to be a stockholder, or refuse to act, ol any director, it shall be in the power
of the board of directors to fill up the vacancy occasioned thereby.

Sec 4- And be it enacted, That the said

president and directors shall have power and authority to receive endowments of personal or mixed property for a term of years in trust, to grant annuities, to make insurances on lives, to contract for reversionary payments, to make all kinds of contracts in which the casualties of life, and interest of money are involved, to provide for the investment of funds of the corporation in such manner as they shall deem most safe and beneficial, and generally to pass all such by-laws as

may be necessary to carry this law into effect, not contrary to the laws of the United States or of this state, and from

time to time to alter or repeal the same; and to make, execute and perfect, such and so many contracts, bargains,

agreements, and other instruments, as shall or may be necessary and as the nature of the case shall or may require.

Sec. 5. And be it enacted, That all contracts, policies, and other instruments of writing, not under seal, made by said president and directors, shall be good and valid in law and equity.

Sec. 6. And be it enacted, That no transfer of stock shall he made but in person, or by attorney, in writing, on the books of said corporation, and with the consent of said president and directors thereof, and no stockholder indebted to said corporation shall be permitted to transfer his or her stock until the debts due by him or her to said corporation shall be fully paid and satisfied.

Sec. 7. And be it enacted, That, it shall be the duty of the president and directors, on the first Monday in March in every year, or within ten days thereafter, to appoint from the stockholders three competent persons as a committee of examination, whose duty it shall be to investigate the affairs of the company, and to make a report thereof; and the president and directors shall keep full, fair and correct entries of their proceedings, which shall at all times be open to the inspection of the stockholders.

Sec. 8. And be it enacted, That it shall be the duty of said president and directors to make dividends of the profits of said corporation on the first Monday in January and July annually.

Sec. 9. And be it enacted, That no stockholder shall be liable for any debts, contracts, nor engagements of said corporation, but that the money, property, rights and credits, of the company, shall alone be liable for the same.

Sec. 10. And be it enacted. That the president and directors may at any time call a meeting of the stockholders of said company, giving at least three weeks notice in two or more daily newspapers published in the city of Baltimore, and any number of stockholders, owning not less than three hundred shares, may at any time apply to the said president and directors to call a general meeting for any purpose relative to said corporation, and if the said president and directors refuse, any number of stockholders, owning not less than three hundred shares aforesaid, shall have power to call a general meeting, giving the notice aforesaid in the manner aforesaid, and specifying in such notice the object of the meeting; and the resolutions passed at such meeting, by the concurrence of stockholders

Sec. 12. And be it enacted, That nothing in this act contained shall be construed to restrict the right of the legislature, which is hereby reserved in its fullest extent, to impose from time to time, and at all times hereafter, and levy such reasonable tax, by license or otherwise, upon all the property, estate and funds, in which the capital stock of said company shall be invested, in common with similar property, estate or funds, of any other company, corporation, or individuals of this state.

Sec. 13. And be it enacted. That this act shall continue and he in force until the year eighteen hundred and sixty,
and until the end of the session of the general assembly which shall be thereafter.

Source:
Archives of Maryland, Electronic Edition, Maryland State Archives, V. 153 Chap. 149

Baltimore Life Insurance Company
Officers and Agents[1]

Presidents

John I. Donaldson	1830-66
William G. Harrison	1866-67

Secretaries

George Carr Grundy	1830-33?
William Murdoch	1838?-45
Richard B. Dorsey	1845-53
Henry F. Thompson	1854-55
A. B. Coulter	1856-60
M. M. Coulter	1860-61
F. M. Colston	1861-62
J. Colston	1862-65
William M. Dickson	1866-67

Agents

<u>Annapolis, MD</u>

Somerville Pinckney	1833-??
Cornelius McLean	1842-48?

<u>Charleston, SC</u>

J. J. Miller	1841-??

<u>Fredericksburg, VA</u>

Dr. Beverly R. Wellford	1833-54
J. S. Wellford	1854-60
C. B. Wellford	1860-65

---

[1] This list is not intended as a complete list of all officers and agents of the Baltimore Life Insurance Company. The specific dates of service, particularly for the agents, are approximations.

Hagerstown, MD
  William B. Clarke   1848?-??
Hartford, CT
  Thomas C. Perkins   1835-36?
Leesburg, VA
  George Richards   1833-37?
Louisville, KY
  F. W. Geisendorff & Co. 1835-39
  Simeon S. Goodwin   1839-46?
Lynchburg, VA
  Charles L. Mosby   1837-65
Maysville, KY
  John C. Dervees   1846?-55?
New York, NY
  Benjamin S. Whitney   1847-48?

Norfolk, VA
  Robertson & Branda   1835-56
  (discontinued)   1856
Petersburg, VA
  William F. Davis   1838-40?
  R. Ritchie   ??-1842
  (discontinued)   1842-45
  W. E. Hinton   1845-??
  R. F. Lester   1859-63
Richmond, VA
  John O. Lay   1833-40
  C. H. Baldwin   1840-42
  (discontinued)   1842-??
  Corydon H. Sutton   1851-52
  John Darracott   1853-56
  P. B. Price   1856-60
  Lucien Lewis   1860-61

<u>Washington, D.C.</u>

James H. Causten	1833-46
Charles W. Pairo	1846-57
John W. Magill	1858-65

Baltimore American and Commercial Advertiser
January 2 1832

Appendix 2.

The Taney Papers
Application of Roger B. Taney
Death Certificate of Roger B. Taney

BALTIMORE LIFE INSURANCE COMPANY.

APPLICATION FOR LIFE INSURANCE.

(Questions to be answered by the Applicant.)

Question. When and where were you born?

Answer. *I was born in Calvert County in the state of — Maryland on the seventeenth day of March Seventeen hundred and seventy seven.*

Question. Where do you now reside, and what is your condition or employment?

Answer. *I reside in the city of Baltimore, & am the chief Justice of the Supreme court of the United States.*

Question. Are you now in good health, and do you usually enjoy good health, or how otherwise?

Answer. *I am now in good health, & have enjoyed good health for some years last past—although my constitution is not what would be termed robust.*

Question. Has your family been liable to any serious disease—such as Consumption, Insanity, Scrofula, &c.

Answer. — *No.*

Question. Have you at any time been afflicted with Insanity, Gout, Asthma, Consumption, Scrofula, Convulsions, Palsy, or any other disease likely to impair your constitution?

Answer. *No.*

Question. Have you had any wound, hurt, or serious bodily injury? and what?

Answer. *No.*

Question. Have you been vaccinated or had the Small-Pox?

Answer. *I have had the Small pox.*

Question. Are you of a sedentary turn, or accustomed to much exercise?

Answer. *I am accustomed to exercise freely by walking & riding.*

Question. Do you know of any circumstance which renders an insurance on your life more than usually hazardous?

Answer. no. -

(*Declaration to be signed by the Applicant.*)

I, *Roger B. Taney* of the *city of Baltimore* intending to make insurance with the Baltimore Life Insurance Company, in the sum of *five thousand dollars* upon my own life for *for life* do hereby agree, that the answers which I have given to the foregoing questions be the basis of the contract between the said Company and me; and that if any untrue averment be contained in said answers, all moneys which shall have been paid to the Company upon account of insurance made in consequence thereof, shall be forfeited, and the contract made by the said Company shall be void.

At the *City of Baltimore* this *ninth* day of *October* one thousand eight hundred and thirty *eight.*

R. B. Taney

(*Questions to be answered by the family physician, or other respectable physician, or, in case neither can be had, by any known respectable persons in the neighbourhood.*)

Question. Do you know *Roger B. Taney* mentioned in the above application, and how long have you known *him*?

Answer. I have known him intimately for several years

Question. When did you see *him* last?

Answer. a few days ago

Question. Is the said *R. B. Taney* sober and temperate, or are *his* habits such as usually tend to shorten life?

Answer. He is in all respects discreet in his habits and careful of his health

Question. Is there any constitutional disease in *his* family? and what?

Answer. None that I know of

Question. Do you believe that the answers given by the applicant to the questions proposed on the preceding page are correct and well founded, or in what respects are they otherwise?

Answer. I know nothing to the contrary

John Buckler

127

Balto Dec 5th 1864

John I Donaldson Esqr
    Dear Sir
        We enclose you a Certificate
of the death of the late Chief Justice Taney
furnished us by his attending physician
and beg to know when the Company, of
which you are President, will be ready
to pay the amount of the policy on his
life effected by him with it.
    We are Sir
        Yours most Respy
        David M. Perine
        I. Mason Campbell
        Executors of the late
        Roger B. Taney —

Other Heritage Books by Jerry M. Hynson:

Absconders, Runaways and Other Fugitives in the
Baltimore City and County Jail

Baltimore [Maryland] City Jail War Docket

Baltimore Life Insurance Company Genealogical Abstracts

District of Columbia Runaway and Fugitive Slave Cases, 1848–1863

Free African-Americans Maryland, 1832: Including Allegany, Anne Arundel,
Calvert, Caroline, Cecil, Charles, Dorchester, Frederick, Kent,
Montgomery, Queen Anne's, and St. Mary's Counties

Maryland Freedom Papers, Volume 1: Anne Arundel County

Maryland Freedom Papers, Volume 2: Kent County

Maryland Freedom Papers, Volume 3: Maryland Colonization
Society Manumission Book, 1832–1860

The African American Collection: Anne Arundel County, Maryland
Marriage Licenses, 1865–1888

The African American Collection: Cecil County, Maryland
Indentures, 1777–1814

The African American Collection: Kent County, Maryland
Marriages, 1865–1888